A Guide to the C. S. Lewis Tour in Oxford

A Guide to the C. S. Lewis Tour in Oxford

A step by step guide that will explain how to find 'the Kilns', the former home of Clive Staples Lewis in Oxford and lots more...

Ronald K. Brind

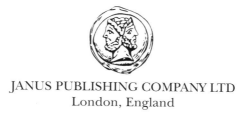

JANUS PUBLISHING COMPANY LTD
London, England

First Published in Great Britain 2005
by Janus Publishing Company Ltd,
93–95 Gloucester Place,
London W1U 6JQ

www.januspublishing.co.uk

British Library Cataloguing-in-Publication Data
A catalogue record for this book
is available from the British Library

ISBN 978-1-85756-626-0

Cover Design: Nathan Cording
Photographs: Ronald K. Brind

Printed and bound in Great Britain

To my parents William and Ellen Brind, who instilled in me honesty, civility and common sense values and who unstintingly cared for me during my childhood years and beyond.

Also to my wife Anna Brind (née Tackley), our son Andrew Brind, his wife Julia (née Gurden) and their children Charlotte and Matthew Brind. To our daughter Sarah Jayne Plows, her husband Christopher and their children Jamie Shepherd, Emily Shepherd and Michael Ronald Plows.

Contents

Acknowledgements

This book was written with the help and encouragement of many people to whom I am extremely grateful. I would therefore like to thank them publicly, they are; my wife Anna, children Andrew Keith and Sarah Jayne for their love and support; my parents Ellen and William Brind, who are in safe hands watching over me; the Rev. Tom Honey, Vicar of Holy Trinity Church, for his kind permission to use information from Voirrey Carr's 'History of the Building' and the transcription of the Rev. Canon R. E. Head's tape, titled *Two People of the Foothills*, also for a set of keys to Holy Trinity Church in order that I can accompany the many C. S. Lewis followers who make the pilgrimage to see Tom's deserved piece of history; to Humphrey Carpenter for his excellent book *The Inklings*; David Bratman for his book, *A Beginner's Bibliography of the Inklings*; my friends Jean Wakeman, Douglas and Merrie Gresham; Eileen Roberts, Director of Alumnae Relations, St Hilda's College, Magdalen College School; the Nuffield Orthopaedic Centre, the Oxford Mail, the Southern California Christian Examiner, 'Crippin', Walter Hooper, Rick and Manuel Hernandez from Atlanta, USA, the former named being responsible for the suggestion that I write this book after completing the tour during 2003.

Rick and Manuel Hernandez travelled from Atlanta, Georgia, USA, to Oxford, England, to experience the C. S. Lewis Tour, but without them saying how much they had enjoyed the tour and that for them it was the 'last piece of the puzzle' because they had seen *Shadowlands* many times and read everything Lewis had written, I

1

probably would not have written this book. They said, 'You should write a book about your childhood memories of the Kilns.' The following extracts are taken from a letter from Rick after they had been on the tour during April 2003:

> Well, first of all C. S. Lewis was a batchelor for most of his life and I can relate to that because although I am only thirty-one, I have been alone for most of my adult life as well. The fact that C. S. Lewis was a great scholar and tutor at Oxford really interests me because I attended Oxford for a short time and learned the love of reading and the written word. The whole story of Jack losing Joy to cancer took on a new significance last year when Manuel and I lost our mother to cancer. It was very painful and our mother suffered for about two years, with the last six months being the worst. During the whole experience with my mother, I would think about Jack and how he felt of losing Joy, someone he loved very much. I was first introduced to C. S. Lewis in watching the film *Shadowlands* and that's where my love of his life and writings began, so you can see why I had great interest in your tour. You have an important story to tell and that is really extraordinary! The only thing I can say is that the only thing better than the tour itself was to have met you, a person who was there when it happened.
>
> Rick Hernandez

Introduction

This guide is written in such a way that it will allow the reader with minimal knowledge of Oxford's roads and/or the former haunts of Clive Staples Lewis the opportunity to do the 'C. S. Lewis Tour' with very little other help required.

A comprehensive list of 'landmark photographs' can be found at the rear of this guide, with 'tick' boxes and room to record date's and your comments etc., acting as your diary for the day. The photographs will also help you to recognise your location with regard to your progress, along with the taxi driver 'take me there' list that follows.

Taxi driver 'take me there' list

1. Beaumont Street – The Randolph Hotel, The Ashmolean Museum. 10 minutes

2. St Giles — Martyrs Memorial, St Johns College and The Eagle and Child. 15 minutes

3. Banbury Road – enroute to Parks Road.

4. Parks Road – Keble College and the Natural History Museum. 5 minutes

5. South Parks Road – Rhodes House. 5 minutes

6. St Cross Road – St Cross Church and Cemetary. 20 minutes

7. Longwall Street – Old City Wall and Magdalen College 'battlement style' wall. 5 minutes

8. High Street – Magdalen College, Magdalen Great Tower, Magdalen Bridge, Punting on the River Cherwell. 20 minutes

9. The Plain – enroute to Cowley Place.

10. Cowley Place – Magdalen College School and St Hilda's College. 10 minutes

11. St Clements Street – enroute to Headington Road.

12. Headington Road – enroute to Sandfield Road.

13. Sandfield Road – J.R.R. Tolkien's former home. 5 minutes

14. London Road – enroute to Old High Street.

15. Old High Street – Joy Davidman's former home. 5 minutes

16. NOC, Windmill Road – Formerly the Wingfield Hospital and Mayfair Suite. 10 minutes (Data Protection Act – be careful not to include members of the public in your photographs)

17. Old Road – enroute to Quarry Road.

18. Quarry Road – enroute to Quarry Hollow.

19. Quarry Hollow – enroute to Quarry School Place.

20. Quarry School Place – enroute to Trinity Road.

21. Trinity Road – Holy Trinity Church, Lewis Pew, Churchyard and Lewis grave/tombstone. 30 minutes

22. Eastern Bypass – enroute to Risinghurst Estate and Kiln Lane.

23. Kiln Lane – enroute to Lewis Close.

24. Lewis Close – C. S. Lewis' former home, C. S. Lewis Reserve, lake and air-raid shelter. 30 minutes

25. Collinwood Road – The Ampleforth Arms, a former Lewis and Tolkien 'watering hole' and where Dougie and Ron fetched the beer! 5 minutes

26. London Road – enroute to the Northern Bypass.

27. Northern Bypass – enroute to the slip road before the Marston Flyover.

28. Marston Flyover – enroute to Marsh Lane.

29. Marsh Lane – enroute Cherwell Drive.

30. Cherwell Drive – en-route to Marston Ferry Road.

31. Marston Ferry Road - enroute to Banbury Road.

32. Banbury Road – enroute to St Giles.

33. St Giles – enroute to Beaumont Street.

34. Beaumont Street – Return to start point The Randolph Hotel, Oxford.

Oxford's traffic congestion will of course determine your actual times, at any of the locations mentioned, which are provided as a guide only.

The guide also contains history and anecdotes from the 1950s – reflecting on what I believe was probably the most difficult personal period in the life of this so respected man, the knowledge from which you can now benefit by reading before you travel.

The information, directions and my personal opinions contained in this guide will help you to plan a successful and enjoyable visit to the city of Oxford, with memories and thoughts of C. S. Lewis in particular that will last forever! Please remember that it is not possible to gain entry to all of the places mentioned in this guide without prior arrangements being made. The use of a camera is permitted in all of the locations referred to on the C. S. Lewis tour, including Holy Trinity Church and Oxford Crematorium, but remember the Data Protection Act whilst on the Nuffield Orthopaedic Hospital property.

If you arrive in Oxford by train intent on walking to the Randolph Hotel in Beaumont Street for the start of the tour, allow an extra fifteen minutes to walk from the rail station via Hythe Bridge Street for what will be a minimum three-hour experience of a lifetime! On the other hand if you arrive by coach, then Oxford's bus/coach station in George Street is just three minutes away from the Randolph Hotel, via Gloucester Place. Driving your own vehicle into Oxford is not recommended because parking, is to say the least, very difficult, and can work out expensive.

Note: Toilets/restroom facilities are only available en route in hotels, shops and other public areas and restrictions may apply at the weekend. You are also reminded not to leave valuable items such as cameras or handbags on view in your car whilst it is unattended and, finally, don't forget to secure the vehicle, including the windows.

Summary

I honestly believe that the C. S. Lewis Tour came into being by fate. Having experienced the greed of others during my six years in the electronics industry and my patented technology that was going to make me 10 million dollars as we floated the company having been taken from under my nose in an instant, I was left with nothing. As there was now an urgent need to provide for my family, I started driving taxis in Oxford city and it was here that I was approached by two American visitors who asked whether I knew where the former home of C. S. Lewis was situated. I responded, 'Boy, have you struck gold', and proceeded to tell everything that I knew about my time at the Kilns with the Lewis family, including C. S. Lewis (Jack) and Douglas Gresham (Dougie).

Dougie is the biological son of William and Joy Gresham (née Davidman), who would later become one of the two stepsons of C. S. Lewis. The rest of the household included Helen Joy Davidman (Joy), Warren Hamilton Lewis (the elder brother of C. S. Lewis, who was always referred to as Warnie), David Gresham (who was Douglas' older brother), Frank Paxford (Fred), Mrs Miller the housekeeper, a ginger cat and the huge shaggy poodle dog that completed what really was a typical English household of that period.

I was born on 3rd November 1945 to William and Ellen Brind at 6 Grovelands Road, Risinghurst Estate, Headington, Oxford. At fifty-eight years of age, I am today about the same age that Clive Staples Lewis was when he became involved with a lady from America called Helen Joy Davidman. My home was just one hundred and fifty yards away from the 'clay hills', now recognised the world over as the Kilns, an eight-acre plot of typically English cottage and woodland that was the former Oxfordshire home of C. S. Lewis, from 1930 until his death in 1963. The Kilns was the name given to the whole plot rather than just the house as is suggested today. As the name also suggests there were in fact two brick kilns on the site where a brick industry had prevailed for many years and where members of my own family, during the late nineteenth century, would dig their own clay, and form their own bricks which were then fired in the brick kilns. The former Lewis home was built during 1922 but it was 1930 before Mrs Janie King-Moore purchased it for three thousand, three hundred pounds. It was later extended by adding two extra rooms but it was to be Jack's home address until his death in 1963. This wonderland called 'the Kilns' will remain etched in my mind forever and for many different reasons – reasons which will soon become apparent. Clive Staples Lewis, who didn't particularly like the name 'Clive', actually preferred that he be called 'Jacksy' or 'Jacksie' during his own schooldays in Ireland. Over the years 'Jacksy' became 'Jacks' and then 'Jack' but how did the nickname actually come about? There appear to be three possible explanations. 1) After a dearly loved pet dog of his called 'Jacksy' or 'Jacksie' was run over and killed by a motorised vehicle in Ireland, Lewis chose to remember the dog by insisting thereafter that he be called by the same name. 2) As a very young child, possibly three or four years old, he ran to his mother thumping his own chest declaring 'Me called Jacksy', thereafter refusing to respond to any other name. 3) As a young child he became friendly with a train driver in Ireland by the name of Jacksy and insisted on being called by the same name. My own opinion is that the first explanation seems to be the most likely.

Although it is said that Lewis spent much of his life in the home that Dougie and I were fortunate enough to be allowed to play in after school was over, the reality is that he probably spent more time in his rooms at Magdalen College, Oxford, thus occupying the Kilns just some weekends and holidays during the 1950s. Warnie, on the other hand, spent far more time there.

During 1955, as a ten-year-old boy, I would walk the short distance from my parents' semi-detached house to the freedom of the clay hills with fishing rods and a shotgun, to fish and shoot in what we know today as the Kilns, an area of land that was full of tall trees, such as pine, elm, horse chestnut, sycamore, oak and beech. It even had its own lake and air-raid shelter! The floor of the woodland was covered with a leaf mould that was spongy underfoot yet boasting its fair share of fern bracken, brambles and stinging nettles. It was an invitation to explore but there was always the fear of what was underneath the fern bracken that was so tall that it brushed our waistline – a snake perhaps?

The two new boys Douglas and David Gresham moved into the Kilns about 1957, it was soon after that I would look forward to visiting my new friend Dougie to swap stamps, coins and cigarette cards, as well as being allowed to continue shooting in the woodland and fishing in the lake at the back of the house. In those days, at the tender age of just ten years, it was legal to purchase a shotgun licence from the local post office, as well as own and carry a shotgun in the street with a pocket full of cartridges! The shotgun licence would have cost us ten shillings each then – the equivalent today of just fifty pence – and it was valid for a whole year. In those days, and although it was illegal, we would carry a shotgun in the street without it even being covered with a sleeve or in a gun case. I remember the penalty for such an offence – in the unlikely event that you were stopped and prosecuted by the police – was two pounds. I remember the local 'bobby' or Parish policeman was a man called Mr Keep, who lived on Risinghurst and of which the mere sight of his uniform would send shudders through my body, yet I had done nothing wrong. In those days the local policeman was a well-respected member of the community whose presence gave a distinct feeling of safety.

My first shotgun was a twenty-eight-inch double-barrelled .410 bore with very difficult hammers that had to be pulled back to make the gun ready for firing. I remember standing struggling with the gun in the brick-drying barn, opposite Dougie's bedroom. It was quite a challenge but I always pointed the barrels away from anything or anybody in case my thumb slipped off either of the hammers that were draining the muscles in my hand of all strength. Sometimes I would catch a glimpse of one or both of the two grumpy-looking old men, each wearing a long gabardine style mackintosh and a Trilby hat, walking to or from the house; Jack and Warnie turned out to be in fact, anything but grumpy, as they put up with the antics of us boys forever looking for mischief. Who would have thought then that nearly fifty years later I would be writing about my personal knowledge of the Lewis family and the Kilns, which at the time really was taken for granted.

During those days the residents living in the Parish of Risinghurst had little idea that the Kilns had previously been purchased by Mrs Janie King-Moore and Jack wasn't known to the locals as the owner either. Indeed, if either of the brothers were labelled as being the owner it was Warnie, who had retired from the Army in 1932. Hence the property called the Kilns was known to the locals as Major Lewis' house.

This travel guide reflects on those days and allows those who are unable to visit Lewis' typically English country home in person, the opportunity to travel with another 'white stag' but this time in a land of reality.

For those who wish to find out more about C. S. Lewis' life during the 1950s and participate in an accompanied tour, the 'white stag' leaves from outside the Randolph Hotel in Beaumont Street, Oxford, daily. The tour will take you on a journey of a lifetime to experience some of Lewis' former haunts and the fantastic sites that Oxford has to offer but about which little is known by its own residents! All tours have to be pre-booked via the Oxford telephone number +44 (0) 1865 874 500. My website www.cslewistours.com provides information regarding the vehicular tour and, of course, the 'white stag' is the white minibus that I use. My cell phone number is 0792 9032 564 or you can contact me by email through the www.cslewistours.com website.

To complete the tour you will need to allow at least three hours but your itinerary can be easily determined by taking note of the suggested viewing time at each site for photographs and discussion.

Access to the Kilns (today, meaning Lewis' former home)

For information regarding access to the Kilns contact the Head Resident on +44 (0) 1865 741 865. This is a direct line to the Kilns in the United Kingdom for all viewing appointments regarding the former home of C. S. Lewis. However, don't hold your breath whilst you wait for an appointment because, sadly, it appears to be the last priority on the agenda of the C. S. Lewis Foundation based in Redlands, California, and who own the former Lewis property.

Hotel Accommodation at www.picturesofengland.com (official sponsors of *The C. S. Lewis Tour in Oxford*)

Internet services offering discounted hotels and guest house accommodation is available throughout the United Kingdom at picturesofengland.com. Hotel and other accommodation can easily be booked online in advance of your visit at www.picturesofengland.com/hotels/ one of the internet's fastest-growing sites. Currently with 7 million visitors per year www.picturesofengland.com/hotels/ also list a comprehensive directory of attractions, leisure activities, pictures, famous Britons and much more. email: uk2@picturesofengland.com

Bus and Coach Services
Stagecoach – The 'Oxford Tube'

Telephone: +44 (0) 1865 772 250
www.oxfordtube.com

The 'Oxford Tube' operates out of Oxford's Gloucester Green (pronounced Glosta Green), in George Street and has a regular service (every ten minutes) to and from London. It is just as easy to access at the London end with stops at Shepherds Bush, Notting Hill

Gate, Marble Arch and Victoria (the tube actually stops three hundred yards this side of Victoria Station). At Buckingham Palace Road/Grosvenor Gardens you will find the 'Oxford Tube' preparing for the return journey to Oxford. The fleet of twenty-eight coaches will cater for your journey to Oxford in style. The Gloucester Green terminus is just a three-minute walk away from Oxford's city centre or the Randolph Hotel in Beaumont Street, from where the C. S. Lewis Tour starts.

The Oxford Bus Company

The 'Oxford Espress' (X90) from Oxford to London Victoria, 'The Airline' (X70) Oxford to Heathrow and 'The Airlines' (X80) Oxford to Gatwick operate out of Gloucester Green in George Street, Oxford, also. For further details refer to the websites listed below.

Telephone: +44 (0) 1865 785 400
www.oxfordbus.co.uk and www.theairline.info

Police – For information and help
Thames Valley Police Headquarters

Telephone: 08458 505 505
In case of an emergency, wherever you are calling from, in the UK dial 999.

Clive Staples Lewis (1898–1963)

Clive Staples Lewis was born on 29th November 1898 in a village called Strandtown, Belfast, Northern Ireland, to parents Albert J. Lewis, a Lawyer (1863–1929) and Florence (Flora) Augusta Hamilton Lewis (1862–1908).

During 1905, the Lewis family were living in a new home which they had secured on the outskirts of Belfast in Northern Ireland but sadly it would be just three short years before Clive Staples Lewis and his older brother, born on 16th June 1895, Warren Hamilton Lewis (Warnie) would lose their mother to cancer. Flora died on her husband Albert's birthday, 23rd August 1908, at the age of forty-six years; their father would live for another twenty years. It happened that soon after their mother's death the two boys were sent away to boarding school in England which Jack was not impressed with. He hated the strict rules and the less than sympathetic masters and missed Belfast tremendously, but in a twist of fate the school closed in 1910, thus Jack was on his way back home to Ireland! He attended several schools and colleges throughout Ireland and England and discovered a love of poetry and modern languages before securing a scholarship and being accepted at University College, Oxford. University College, Oxford, is the city's oldest college, having been founded by William of Durham in 1249.

As an eighteen-year old, during 1916, Lewis lived at 1 Mansfield Road, Oxford, and surely by coincidence J. R. R. Tolkien was lodging at 99 Holywell Street; quite literally they lodged just around the corner from each other. Having settled into his digs in Oxford, Jack began his academic studies at University College before joining the British Army just six months later for active duty during the First World War. Soon, as was the case with so many other young men, Lewis was fighting in the muddy trenches of northern France, and although injured during 1918 returned to duty before getting his discharge in 1919. Lewis then returned to University College, Oxford.

In 1925, at the tender age of just twenty-seven years, and after graduating with first-class honours in Greek and Latin Literature, Philosophy and Ancient History and English Literature, Lewis was elected Fellow at Magdalen College, Oxford, where he taught English Language and Literature for the next twenty-nine years. From student, to professor of Medieval and Renaissance Literature (Magdalene College, Cambridge, in 1955), Lewis the author is renowned for his writing of letters, poems, academic works, novels, science fiction and fantasy with so many books dealing with a vast range of subjects including Christianity, for which he is probably best known. Lewis' first major work, *The Pilgrims Regress'* (1933, was about his own spiritual journey.

During 1931 and after having talked at length with J. R. R. Tolkien, who was a devout Roman Catholic, and Hugo Dyson, Lewis became a Christian again. In a book written by Lewis, *Surprised by Joy,* he refers to the day that he and Warnie travelled to Whipsnade Zoo on a motorcycle. As they departed from Oxford Jack didn't believe that Jesus Christ was the Son of God but when they got to Whipsnade Zoo, near Dunstable, Bedfordshire, he did! 1938 saw the first novel in the space trilogy published, *Out of the Silent Planet* the hero apparently modelled on Lewis' friend J.R.R. Tolkien, followed by *Perelandra* in 1943 and *That Hideous Strength* in 1945. But lets not forget *The Screwtape Letters,* which were broadcast regularly and where many started to take more notice of Lewis, such that during 1941 *The Guardian,* a religious newspaper, began to publish in weekly instalments which lasted over a period of several months. But sadly *The Guardian* ceased publication during 1951. The money earned by Lewis for his work was often given to charity.

The Lewis story really is one of an exceptionally talented man and one can't help but wonder how he managed so much during his short life.

Lewis left Magdalen College, Oxford, in 1954 for Cambridge, where he was afforded the title Professor, but it would not be long before he was to return to Oxford to spend the remaining years of his life at the Kilns, to then marry a divorced lady from America, a lady whom he grew to love dearly. Lewis resigned his position at Cambridge on 2nd August 1963, just a few months before he died (42nd Anniversary, 2nd August 2005). After his marriage to Joy Davidman in April 1956 and just over four years together as man and wife Joy died on 13th July 1960. Jack was able to write about the pain of losing Joy, before he died during the early evening of 22nd November 1963 at the Kilns. It was also the day that President John F. Kennedy was assassinated in Dallas and the English novelist and essayist Aldous Leonard Huxley died (1894–1963), once a student in Oxford also.

The Clay Hills (known today as the Kilns)

During the mid-1950s, although I was already familiar with the clay hills, two new boys had arrived on the scene. One of the boys, Douglas Gresham, and I got on well together but somehow his older brother David was different. He never wanted to join in with the fun and games, or mischief that Dougie and I got up to and spent most of his time reading and writing in the library. Soon I was invited into the house and brushing past the jacket tails of C. S. Lewis but at the time had no idea of who he was, nor yet the impact that he would make in later years – a man who has changed the hearts and minds of millions of people throughout the world and who continues to do so.

It wasn't long before Dougie had established himself at the Kilns, fishing, shooting and tree climbing, the latter reminding me of his favourite tall tree at the bottom end of the Kilns near the Reservoir, Haines field and a stile, which was a timber construction bridging a muddy footpath leading to Shotover Hill (today a nature reserve). The muddy patch was wet both winter and summer, with water trickling through it from the hills of the Shotover reserve, which can be found towards the rear of the Kilns. Dougie would occupy the top of the tree overlooking the area with a pair of binoculars on a regular basis and sat quietly as a courting couple got down to business in the grass below, completely unaware of Dougie with his binoculars in the tree above. Dougie climbed down from the tree and, with a cigarette between his fingers, wandered over to the couple who were still preoccupied in the grass and oblivious to his presence. You can almost imagine what he said, perhaps something like, 'Excuse me, ah excuse me, can you give me a light for my cigarette please?' He never did tell me what they said in response!!

As for David Gresham, my understanding is that he later followed in the footsteps of his mother in taking up Judaism as was his legal right, has since married and is living in India. It would be nice to meet David again as I haven't seen or heard anything from him since the mid-1950s.

The Survey

I think it is fair to say that C. S. Lewis is one of the most influential writers of our day. It was therefore something of a shock to receive the response that I did in a recent survey carried out in the centre of Oxford for the benefit of this guide.

I approached those groups of people who I considered to be typically 'Brits', looking for the husband and wife team or partners with children and shopping bags that suggested they were local. I always asked the same questions and always in the same manner. The first question was, 'Can you tell me who C. S. Lewis was?' The response I got was unbelievable – they would often look dumbfounded and start clicking their fingers but eventually they offered, 'Ah yes, ah umm, oh, ah!' and then with their knuckles touching their lips they answered *'Alice in Wonderland'*. I responded with, 'No, that was Lewis Carroll, Dodgson, Christ Church College.' 'Oh yes', came the reply and once again they would start searching for an answer. I asked the next question, 'Have you ever heard of, or read, a book called *'The Lion, the Witch and the Wardrobe?'* – to which they would often happily reply, 'Yes'! But having answered my question, the glee on their face would soon disappear as they came back to me with an almost derogatory question, 'Wasn't he the old man, that chap, the old geezer who lived up the Kilns?' I said, 'Yes, that's him, thank you.' Of just under two hundred people that I interviewed and in response to the question, 'Excuse me can you tell me who C. S. Lewis was?'– the exact words in reply in 70 per cent of answers was *'Alice in Wonderland'*! How does that saying go about a prophet in his own city?

Mrs Janie King-Moore (1873–1951)

Mrs Janie King-Moore, who Jack often referred to as 'Minto,' was the lady that purchased the Kilns in 1930. She was nearly twenty-six years Jack's senior and during the early 1920s was living at 14 Holyoake Road, Headington, by coincidence a few hundred yards from where Helen Joy Davidman later lived at 10 Old High Street. However, Jack's moving in with Mrs Moore during 1922 in Headington was a direct result of an agreement between Jack and Paddy Moore, son of Mrs Janie King-Moore, who, before they went off to the Great War and whilst they were roommates at Keble College, Oxford, agreed that in the event of one or the other being killed in action, each would look after the other's family. Sadly, Paddy Moore, aged twenty years, was killed in action and buried in the field in Peronne, Southern France. For some reason, bearing in mind the agreement was between Jack and Paddy, Mrs Moore subsequently honoured the agreement made between them at Keble and effectively inherited two step-sons, or did Jack and Warnie inherit a step-mother? Either way, it was to be the start of a long relationship for all concerned. Mrs Moore also had a daughter called Maureen (1906 – 1997) who was later to become Lady Dunbar of Hempriggs. The small village of Hempriggs is situated approximately thirty-five miles north east of Inverness near Burghead Bay in the Moray Firth, Scotland, a very long way from the Kilns.

Six years after Jack's death, during 1969, an organisation called the Berkshire, Buckinghamshire and Oxfordshire Naturalist Trust, 'BBONT' (pronounced bee'bont), acquired the freehold of the lake and woodland to the rear of the former Lewis home by way of Henry Stephen, who owned the property built in Lewis' back garden. Today BBONT still own the freehold, although after a name change they are known as the Wildlife Trust and are responsible for the upkeep of the so called C. S. Lewis Reserve (in memory of Henry Stephen). Also sold for development by Mrs Janie King-Moore's daughter Maureen and Warnie (Jack's older brother) was the plot of land at the Kilns which I remember as the orchard, where today an additional seven houses stand and which I believe contributed to the demise of the Kilns.

After the death of Mrs Janie King-Moore on 12th January 1951 the Lewis brothers continued to live at the property as per the 'Right of Life Tenancy' that she had previously agreed with them, meaning that they could stay there for as long as they wished even after her death. However, mystery follows regarding Mrs Janie King-Moore's burial, which as yet is still unexplained because she was curiously buried in the same grave in Holy Trinity churchyard as another Mrs Moore, namely Mrs Alice Hamilton Moore, described on her tombstone as widow of Dr Robert Moore of Bush Mills, Ireland. Although there is confusion over why the two women are buried in the same grave, the Burial Register reveals that the Irish Mrs Moore buried in 1939 was also recorded as being resident at the Kilns at that time. We know, of course, that Mrs Janie King-Moore purchased the Kilns (meaning the Lewis home) in 1930 but she would hardly have purchased it with a sitting tenant and there is no mention of another Mrs Moore in residence at the Kilns throughout this intriguing story! But by a strange coincidence it seems there could have been another Mrs Moore (the name is even spelt the same way) resident at the Kilns, but living in another property within the eight-acre plot. There is even more intrigue because the name 'Hamilton', as in Alice Hamilton, widow of Dr Robert Moore of Bush Mills, Ireland, and inscribed on the tombstone, is in the Lewis family. For example, Lewis' mother's name was Florence Augusta 'Hamilton' Lewis and then, of course, there was Warren 'Hamilton' Lewis. Many theories have been put to me regarding the burial of these two ladies but as yet nothing can be substantiated and although the transcript of a tape referring to the burial recorded by the Rev. R. E. Head, vicar of Holy Trinity Church during the 1950s, is reproduced later in this guide, there is still no satisfactory answer, although I do hope to be able to solve the puzzle one day.

Further recent research suggests that Alice Hamilton Moore was a family friend living in Ireland, who fell upon hard times and thus was offered the facility of the bungalow specially built for her within the Lewis plot. Therefore, when she died she was 'resident' at the Kilns. By the mid-1950s the old wooden bungalow was just a wreck of a building that Dougie and I would play in.

Helen Joy Davidman (1915 – 1960) and the Marriage of Convenience

Helen Joy Gresham (née Davidman) was an American Jewess, poetess and authoress who had been in correspondence with Jack for a number of years. Joy, as she preferred to be known, was the lady that C. S. Lewis would marry, thus Douglas and David Gresham her sons from an earlier marriage, would become step-sons through marriage to C. S. Lewis. As a twelve year-old boy who frequented the Kilns during the mid-1950s on a regular basis, I can now look back and consider myself the fortunate one to be allowed into the home of Lewis, although strangely I never knowingly saw Joy in the house. In fact, the only time I ever recall seeing Joy, apart from their week-ends away that is, was outside the house one sunny summer evening when both Jack and Joy were sitting on a blanket that had been laid across the lawn beyond the rose-covered rustic fence at the rear of the property. I never saw her chasing after Dougie as most mothers would, telling him to clean up his bedroom, for example, so now when I think back and wonder why, I can only suggest that as her illness was diagnosed six months after their marriage in 1956 and bearing in mind that she moved into the Kilns during 1957, she must have spent a lot of her time in hospital and/or was confined to her bedroom. Consider also that holidays in Ireland, Greece and week-ends away at Studley Priory Hotel in Horton-cum-Studley, a nearby Oxfordshire village were the probable reasons for my not seeing much of her. Clive Staples Lewis and Helen Joy Davidman were married in the Oxford Registry Office on 23rd April 1956. The building is situated at the corner of Tidmarsh Lane and New Road, Oxford (not on the C. S. Lewis Tour route). It was considered at the time by most to be a marriage of convenience to stop the British Immigration Authority deporting Joy because her visa was about to expire. I personally consider it was a very brave thing for Jack to do during those years unlike perhaps today, because being involved with a divorced lady was almost unheard of and it would most certainly have been frowned upon by many of Lewis' friends.

It was six months into their marriage, on 19th October 1956, that Joy was diagnosed as suffering from cancer. She was subsequently admitted to the Wingfield Hospital in Windmill Road, Headington, less than half a mile away from where she was living in Old High Street, Headington. In a book called *Lenten Lands,* written by Douglas Gresham, he recalls the occasion as he walked through the main entrance of the Wingfield Hospital to visit his mother, Jack having told him that they were going to visit his mother with a broken leg! So, even at this early stage in their relationship, I believe Jack was trying to protect Dougie from the awful truth.

During December 1956 and because Joy's death from cancer was believed to be imminent, their marriage was blessed by a clergyman at her bedside. The Ceremony took place in the Mayfair Suite of the Wingfield Hospital in Headington, rather than a London hospital as we are encouraged to believe in that brilliant film called *Shadowlands.* Soon after the ceremony, Joy made what has been described as a remarkable recovery and by April 1957 was living with Jack at his home, up at the Kilns. However, their time together as man and wife would be short-lived because, on 13th July 1960, Joy died of the cancer in the Radcliffe Infirmary in Woodstock Road, Oxford – she was just forty-five years of age. Jack was devastated and wrote about his feelings after her death in *A Grief Observed* which was published under the pseudonym of N. W. Clerk. Dougie, who I had never heard complain and who never told me that his mother was suffering from a serious illness, must have been absolutely distraught. Of the two brothers, I believe it was probably David, the older of the two boys, who was already struggling to shoulder the burden of their parents' earlier divorce and now the death of their mother. Little did the boys realise that they would lose their biological father also in less than two years! Thinking back, my own opinion now is that the events unfolding at the time were the probable reason for David's quiet, even apathetic manner. But, of course, we were all three young boys and in those days there would not have been the support available that there is today.

William Lindsay Gresham (1909–1962)

William Lindsay Gresham was the biological father of brothers Douglas and David Gresham. He was born on 20th August 1909 in Baltimore, USA. Gresham had a literary talent of his own, with articles being published on a regular basis. *Nightmare Alley* (1946) is probably the title that would likely come to mind for some, although I suspect others would struggle to even recognise the name. Both William and Joy Gresham had been long-serving members of the Communist Party during which time Joy had a book of poetry published called *Letters to a Comrade*. In a sudden change of direction they joined the Presbyterian Church but William Gresham had become a violent man with alcohol playing a major part in his life. It was during 1953 that William Gresham wrote to Joy admitting to a relationship with her cousin Renee Rodriguez. Renee was herself also married with two children, but was soon to become the third wife of William Gresham.

Joy went back to America in an attempt to resolve matters with her husband but to no avail; their divorce followed. In 1954 William Gresham and Renee Rodriguez were married in Florida but as has been the case throughout this intriguing Gresham/Davidman/Lewis love story, their marriage was to be short-lived also. In 1960, after learning of Joy's death, Gresham visited England to see his sons Douglas and David. His opinion was simply that they should stay in England with the Lewis brothers and he returned to America. But soon after his return he discovered that he too was suffering from a life-threatening illness; he also had been diagnosed as having cancer but rather than suffer the experience of a slow death from cancer as the disease took hold Gresham committed suicide in a somewhat squalid 'Dixie' hotel room on 14th September 1962, where he had booked in as Asa Kimball of Baltimore. Gresham had previously written about Asa Kimball in a novel called *Limbo Towers* (1949).

Predominant Works of C. S. Lewis

C. S. Lewis is best known to his millions of followers throughout the world for a number of works, not least the following examples, a few of my own favourites.

The Screwtape Letters – A series in which Jack writes letters from one devil to another.

Mere Christianity – Here Jack writes about Christianity and why we should believe in it.

Surprised by Joy – Recalls how he converted to Christianity.

The Problem of Pain – Lewis attempts to explain why God allows us all to suffer.

A Grief Observed – Was published under a pseudonym in 1960 and relates to a diary that Jack kept after the death of his wife Joy from cancer.

Letters to Malcolm – Here he writes about devotion to an imaginary friend.

The Chronicles of Narnia – The following titles are in the order in which they were first published:

The Lion, the Witch and the Wardrobe (1950)

Prince Caspian (1951)

The Voyage of the Dawn Treader (1952)

The Silver Chair (1953)

The Horse and His Boy (1954)

The Magicians Nephew (1955)

The Last Battle (1956)

There are, of course, many, many more and each of us no doubt has our own favourite and for various reasons, but I think the title most discussed and appreciated, certainly in my company whilst doing the tours, is *Mere Christianity*.

The Four Loves

The Four Loves (1960) – In this book Lewis refers to love and affection, friendship and charity.

There is no doubt in my mind that Jack contributed to all four love, affection, friendship and charity but I think most would agree he was a deep thinker! So could it be that he did actually have four loves during his lifetime? Although some avid readers of Lewis' *The Four Loves* will no doubt say he didn't mean it that way, I suggest you might like to consider the following. We know that he was very close to his mother, and there have been questions about a relationship with Mrs Janie King-Moore. We know about Joy Davidman, of course, but what do we know about a 'fourth' love that he may have been trying to tell us about in the title *The Four Loves*, and who might it have been – if indeed there was someone else?

Was Lewis the celibate man that we all thought he was? Is it possible that he did have feelings for another lady? I was told by a group of Americans who did the C. S. Lewis Tour one day (I have been unable to substantiate this yet), that he refers in one of his books, or perhaps a book written about him, to the fact that he 'could' have or 'wanted' to marry another lady although they were unable to name the title. As I have not read everything that he wrote, I look forward to finding it!

However, the fact is I remember a lady visiting the Kilns on a very regular basis during the 1950s. She was attractive, young and involved in publishing, writing and journalism, working from London with some strong political views, so you could say she had the right 'credentials', if it were to be relevant, to match the intellectual Lewis. She was also responsible for test driving and reporting on fast cars at the time.

During December 2003, whilst I was searching for information about the former estate after the death of Warren Hamilton Lewis, I actually came across a copy of his Last Will and Testament. In it various bequests were made, of course, but the one that interested particularly was in a Codicil to the Will dated 25th June 1969, that of a thousand pounds to Miss Jean Wakeman. The name suddenly rang a bell in my head. Yes, I do remember Jean visiting the Kilns on a regular basis and, as it gave a local address, I decided to follow it up to see if there was any trace of her former home, 'The Old Vicarage;' perhaps, if I was really lucky, I might even get a photograph! To my absolute surprise and delight and after several visits to the address, which I had found by chance, I managed to speak to Jean, who lives about four miles away from the Kilns in a small Oxfordshire village called Horton-cum-Studley. After explaining who I was to her nurse, I was invited in and then allowed a few minutes during which time Jean and I recalled our memories of the past. Alas, our meeting was brought to an abrupt end just as it was getting interesting because Jean had a hospital appointment to keep. But before I left I enquired about a recent photograph of Douglas Gresham, his wife Merrie, their children and grandchildren that takes pride of place in the lounge on her sideboard cabinet. Jean then told me that she was Douglas' guardian! I was, to say the least, somewhat surprised by that statement which now had me thinking and wondering – what if? Jean, in her own words during our meeting, said, 'I was on the scene long before Joy Davidman', and she followed that statement with, 'Joy and I became good friends.' My brain was racing, but just as I was going to ask the inevitable question Jean said, 'You must come back and see me another time – I have a hospital appointment to keep.' She then allowed me to have her telephone number, which is ex-directory, and suggested that we meet again. I left the house wondering if Jean Wakeman could have been Lewis' fourth love whom he could have married and perhaps about which even Jean, to this day, has no idea.

I had visited Jean Wakeman just before Christmas 2003 but as time went by I needed to complete the manuscript for this book and still hadn't had the second meeting with her. I decided to take the bull by the horns so to speak, and ask the question over the telephone. During a telephone conversation in June 2004 Jean told me that she had first met Jack after *The Screwtape Letters* and that they met socially thereafter, so I felt the time was right to ask the inevitable question. I said, 'Jean, please dont be offended by my asking, but were you romantically involved with Jack? There was a short pause and then in a very determined voice Jean said, 'I cannot understand the insatiable appetite for the intrusion into Lewis' private life', and followed that by saying that she was 'not prepared to discuss it further'. I guess we shall never know the answer!

Relevant information and places to be Visited or Viewed En Route
(with pronunciation and/or slang in brackets)

The Randolph Hotel

Gloucester Green (pronounced Glosta Green)

The Ashmolean Museum

Martyrs Memorial

St John's College (St John's)

The Eagle and Child (the Bird and Baby)

Inklings (the group of men who put pen to paper at the Eagle and Child)

Undergraduate (student at college who has not taken his first degree)

Keble College (Keble)

Digs in Mansfield Road (Lewis' first accommodation in Oxford)

Flop house (American expression for students, accommodation)

Holywell Street (where J. R. R. Tolkien lodged during 1916)

Rhodes House (Rhodes)

St Cross Church (St Cross)

The old Oxford City Wall

Magdalen College (pronounced Maud'lyn)

Fellow (a member of the Board of Trustees, in this case Magdalen College)

Magdalen Bridge

College ball (a social event for dancing)

The River Cherwell (pronounced Char'well), which flows under Magdalen Bridge

Boater (hat), often worn by students in summer

Punts on the Cherwell (a punt is perhaps best described as a gondola-style boat with no mechanical means of propulsion)

Magdalen College School (MCS)

The former home(s) of John Ronald Reuel Tolkien

Extension or extended (the property has been made bigger)

The former home(s) of Helen Joy Gresham (née Davidman)

The Nuffield Orthopaedic Centre – formerly the Wingfield Hospital (known as the NOC)

Headington Quarry (the Quarry)

Pub (public house)

The Masons Arms (the Masons)

Free house (not tied to a particular brewery for purchase of beers, wines, spirits etc.)

Holy Trinity Church (Quarry Church)

TLC (tender loving care)

Lewis Close (cul-de-sac)

The Clay Hills (the Kilns)

Allotments (garden plots)

Stile (timber construction spanning muddy or wet area to avoid wet feet)

Tradesman's entrance (for trade deliveries such as milk, bread, post etc.)

Loft space (attic)

Parish policeman ('bobby')

The Ampleforth Arms (the Amp)

Quart (two pints imperial measure)

3d pre-decimal coinage = three old pennies. When there were two hundred and forty pennies and twenty shillings to the pound.

Oxford Crematorium (the Crem)

C. S. Lewis Tours start from outside the Randolph Hotel, Beaumont Street, Oxford

The Randolph Hotel, Beaumont Street, Oxford, is open to non-residents but unless you decide to sample the delights of the Morse bar, with delightful manager Ailish Hurley at the helm, or afternoon tea perhaps, then five minutes here for photographs will be sufficient. The Randolph Hotel was designed by William Wilkinson and built in

1864. It is Oxford's premier hotel, associated with many famous names and VIPs from all over the world. Known by many locally is Colin Dexter, who wrote the *Inspector Morse* novels, hence the very popular Morse bar, which is situated in the hotel's lobby to the left, as you approach the hotel reception from Beaumont Street. It is well worth a visit for refreshments and you may even bump into Colin Dexter!

It also happens to be the Randolph Hotel where C. S. Lewis received an honorary Doctor of Letters from Laval University, Quebec, and where some of the filming for *Shadowlands* took place. It may well have been that same occasion when both Jack and Warnie were present to meet with Joy Davidman, who had previously suggested in a letter to Jack that they meet for tea. Joy, on the other hand, was looking for a publisher as well as a home for her family, but famously in the *Shadowlands* film arrived at the Randolph Hotel asking, Anybody here by the name of Lewis? I therefore consider it appropriate that the tour starts from outside the Randolph Hotel but, remember, the distances quoted between the various locations are approximate.

Unless you have pre-booked with C. S. Lewis Tours for the ensuing journey, I would certainly recommend that you hire a taxi to start the tour from outside the Randolph Hotel in Oxford rather than trying to use the local bus service, which would require additional local knowledge and would not allow you as the visitor to get close enough to the locations mentioned. Although your taxi driver will be familiar with the route, he may not be able to answer any of your questions about Lewis-related locations, so please always keep a copy of your tour guide handy as your precise travel instructions and relevant information regarding what you are about to experience.

The Tour Begins

Standing with your back to the Randolph Hotel in Beaumont Street, Oxford, the Ashmolean Museum is situated on the opposite side of the road with Martyrs Memorial, designed by architect Sir George

Gilbert Scott, to your right. The Ashmolean Museum was designed by architect C. R. Cockerell and is Britain's oldest public museum. It is able to boast some of the finest collections in the world but if you decide to take a look inside you will need to leave yourself plenty of time to soak up the fabulous history contained therein. The museum is open Tuesday to Saturday from 10am–5pm, Sunday 2pm–5pm and on Bank Holiday Mondays from 2pm–5pm.

Martyrs Memorial in St Giles, Oxford, was completed in 1843. It stands at the southern end of St Giles, Oxford, and was erected in memory of the three protestant bishops Thomas Cranmer, Nicholas Ridley and Hugh Latimer who were burnt at the stake at the western end of Broad Street, Oxford. Today a cross at the same level as the tarmacadam in the middle of the road indicates the actual site of the ditch, then outside Oxford's north gate, where the deed took place. The reason for pointing out Martyrs Memorial, with its intricate carvings, at this early stage is that when you first see Holy Trinity Church (Quarry Church to the locals) from the outside it appears to be somewhat medieval – apparently designed intentionally this way by Scott and very different to Exeter College, Oxford, and Martyrs Memorial (also designed by Scott). It is not until you see all of Quarry Church both inside and outside that the then popular decorated Gothic style of the fourteenth century becomes apparent.

As you turn to face Martyrs Memorial in the famous St Giles thoroughfare you will probably be wondering already if your photographs will be as spectacular. Travel about fifty yards to the traffic lights and then turn left into St Giles where along on the right about one hundred yards away is St John's College, Oxford. St John's is reputed to be the wealthiest college (financially that is) in Oxford and is said to own land between Oxford and St John's College, Cambridge, which is over eighty miles away and that it is possible to walk from one college to the other without actually stepping off of land that it owns! Opposite St John's College is the equally famous public house called the Eagle and Child known locally as the 'Bird and Baby', which is also owned by St John's College, Oxford, it being a recent acquisition costing somewhere in the region of 1.2 million pounds; St John's College also owns several other public houses in Oxford.

When it became known that the Eagle and Child was for sale during the early part of 2004, I saw it as an excellent opportunity to turn this famous public house into a shrine to C. S. Lewis and consequently sent an email to the C. S. Lewis Foundation of Redlands, California, requesting help to purchase, whilst pointing out that I had previous experience as landlord of a public house and, of course, I was offering the C. S. Lewis Tours. I am still waiting for a response; meanwhile, there is no shrine to C. S. Lewis in Oxford, and no memorabilia shop.

It was at the Eagle and Child during the 1930s that C. S. Lewis would meet with his circle of intellectual friends, collectively known as the Inklings, to discuss each other's written works over a pint of beer, or a pint of cider. Meetings would also take place at his Magdalen College rooms about half a mile away towards Oxford's east gate, hence the Eastgate Hotel for example, just opposite Longwall Street, which used to be another watering hole of both Lewis and Tolkien!

Clearly both Jack and his older brother Warnie enjoyed a glass of beer and/or cider because at the age of about twelve or thirteen years Dougie and I would be handed two empty brown glass cider bottles up at the Kilns and told to get them re-filled with their favourite tipple from the pub called the Ampleforth Arms on Risinghurst. Each bottle held a quart measure (two imperial pints). The Ampleforth Arms, or 'the Amp' as it's known locally, can be seen at 53 Collinwood Road, Risinghurst. My wife and I were tenants of the Amp for a period of time but not, I might add, during the years that John Ronald Reuel Tolkien and Clive Staples Lewis would sit in a back room of the pub over a pint of beer and where, according to one of the older members of the Parish, 'they were often engrossed in conversation that was way above the heads of us locals.' Now that I can believe!

Neither J. R. R. Tolkien nor C. S. Lewis could drive so they would have taken a taxi to each other's homes, which were about two miles apart whilst Tolkien lived in Headington from 1953–1968 and no more than four or five miles apart whilst Tolkien lived at 20 Northmoor Road in Oxford city during the years 1930–47. The latter property referred to is for sale currently at 1.5 million pounds and has an appropriate memorial plaque to record the event.

The Eagle and Child

The Eagle and Child is where the group called the 'Inklings' is generally believed to have originated, but that is not the case. The Inklings as a literary group was first formed by a University College undergraduate in 1931. Today the Eagle and Child is probably best known for the group of men who visited regularly during the 1930s and who between them, in particular J. R. R. Tolkien and C. S. Lewis, are responsible for an understanding of the Christian faith, the like of which we shall probably never see again in our lifetime.

The Eagle and Child has remained in the ownership of University, College, Oxford, since the sixteenth century (until St John's recent purchase that is), but in the 1930s the licensee allowed the Inklings to meet on a Tuesday morning in what is still known as the Rabbit room, a small parlour which today is part of the bar area, although in those days it would have been towards the rear of the pub as the property has been extended considerably since.

Trading as a public house since 1650, it was named after the family of the Earl of Derby. The family crest was a coronet with an eagle and child. Interestingly, during the Civil War the Eagle and Child and the buildings adjacent (now a café and a newsagent) were used as the pay house for Royalist soldiers of Charles I. The chances are that the tenants of these two properties go about their daily business serving coffee and selling newspapers without the slightest knowledge of the history that surrounds them. But during the years 1642–6 Oxford was the capital of Royalist England with Charles I and his Queen Henrietta Maria residing at Christ Church and Merton College respectively.

I am pleased to say that the Lewis' legacy does just about live on at the Eagle and Child with a plaque, photographs and mementoes of the Inklings – a name given to the group as a result of the ink or pen to paper. Sadly, there is no Lewis memorabilia available that I know of either in the Eagle and Child, or anywhere else in Oxford for that matter. You would even struggle to find a bookshop where you could purchase a copy of any of his books, Borders Books at 9 Magdalen St, Oxford, telephone +44 (0)1865 203 901 and Blackwell's at 50 Broad Street, Oxford, being the exceptions, stocking a comprehensive range of titles. (Telephone Blackwell's Bookshop on +44 (0) 1865 792 792.)

There used to be a brewery company trading in Oxford called 'Ind Coope' which was responsible for the heavy wooden pub sign hanging from a bracket on the front wall of the Eagle and Child. It showed a baby held in the claws of the eagle on one side, yet resting between the wings on the reverse. However, it is not the same today! The earlier rectangular sign referred to was gifted to the C. S. Lewis Foundation by Walter Hooper, so if you are ever fortunate enough to gain entry at the Kilns you will see it hanging in the common room, an extension to the former home built in place of the old corrugated tin over timber-framed garage.

For those who wish to refresh themselves, either before or after the tour, the beer and food in the Eagle and Child is good, well presented and reasonably priced. But be warned – toilets en route are few and far between!

I have been asked many times during the tours if there were any women Inklings; the answer is simply that Dorothy L. Sayers is associated in many people's minds with the Inklings' because of her correspondence with both Lewis and Williams, and some similarity in thought.

In listing the names of the group of men called the Inklings, my sincere thanks go to Humphrey Carpenter for his excellent book, *The Inklings,* and to David Bratman for *A Beginner's Bibliography of the Inklings* (http://www.mythsoc.org/inklings.html). Because I am writing primarily about the C. S. Lewis Tour route, I originally put Jack's name first but that would mean that the Lewis brothers' names appeared before that of Tolkien, for example. How could I do that, who would you put first? I solved the problem by listing the Inklings in alphabetical order, leaving you to make up your own mind.

The list of Inklings' names

Barfield, Owen (1898–1997). Philosopher and attorney but considered to be only an occasional visitor at the Inklings' meetings.

Bennett, Jack Arthur Walter (1911–1981). Fellow and tutor at Magdalen College, Oxford, and successor to C. S. Lewis at Cambridge as Professor of Medieval Renaissance English (1964–78).

Cecil, Lord David (1902–1986). English biographer and Professor of English Literature at Oxford.

Coghill, Nevill (1899–1980). Professor of English at Oxford University who also produced plays.

Dundas-Grant, Commander Jim (1896–1985). Commander of the Oxford University Naval Division.

Dyson, Henry Victor 'Hugo' (1896–1975). At Oxford and Reading universities. Lecturer and tutor, buried in St Cross churchyard in Oxford.

Fox, Adam (1883–1977). Professor of Poetry at Oxford (1938–43); Dean of Divinity at Magdalen College, Oxford; Canon of Westminster Abbey.

Hardie, Colin (1906–1998). Oxford University lecturer and tutor in Classics.

Havard, R. E. 'Humphrey' (1901–1985). A physician and author of the clinical appendix to C. S. Lewis' *The Problem of Pain*.

Lewis, Clive Staples (1898–1963). Fellow and tutor in English at Magdalen College, Oxford University (1925–54); Professor of Medieval and Renaissance English at Cambridge University (1954–63). Lewis is buried in Holy Trinity churchyard, Oxford.

Lewis, Warren Hamilton (1895–1973). The older brother of C. S. Lewis, a professional soldier, historian and secretary, to C. S. Lewis in later years, is buried in Holy Trinity churchyard, Oxford.

Mathew, Gervase (1905–1976). Lecturer in Byzantine Studies at Oxford University. Gervase is buried at Wolvercote Cemetery near the grave of J. R. R. Tolkien.

McCallum, R. B. (1898–1973). Lecturer and tutor in Politics and Modern History at Oxford.

Stevens, C. E. 'Tom' (1905–1976). Lecturer and Tutor in Ancient History at Oxford.

Tolkien, Christopher (1924–). Lecturer and tutor in English Language at Oxford (to 1975); son of J. R. R. Tolkien and editor of his father's posthumous works.

Tolkien, John Ronald Reuel (1892–1973). Assistant Editor, *Oxford English Dictionary* (1918–20); Reader (later Professor) of English Language at Leeds University (1920–26); Rawlinson and Bosworth Professor of Anglo-Saxon at Oxford University (1925–45); Merton Professor of English Language and Literature at Oxford University (1945–59). Tolkien is buried, with his wife Edith, at Wolvercote Cemetery about three miles north of Oxford city.

Wain, John (1925–1994). Novelist, poet, dramatist and critic; Professor of Poetry at Oxford University (1973–78).

Williams, Charles Walter Stansby (1886–1945). A prolific author of Theology and Poetry, as well as many other subjects, who joined Oxford University Press as Staff Editor in 1908 and remained there until his death in 1945. Interestingly he always signed his name as just 'Charles Williams'. Williams is buried in St Cross churchyard, Oxford.

Wrenn, Charles (1895–1969). Professor of Anglo-Saxon at Oxford (1946–63).

Dorothy L. Sayers, W. H. Auden, T. S. Eliot and Roger Lancelyn Green, sometimes cited as Inklings, were friends of some of the Inklings but never members of the group. David Lindsay and T. H. White, also sometimes cited as Inklings, had no connection with them whatever.

Unless you decide to eat or have a beer at the Eagle and Child ten minutes is considered plenty of time here for your photographs but be warned, as you face the Eagle and Child poised with your camera the front view looks like something a child might draw during the early days at school – a box with a narrow rectangular door in the middle and elongated windows standing on end at either side. It is advisable to stand at a little bit of an angle to the property before you shoot; you will be a lot happier with the result.

As you leave this fantastic little old English pub, turn left into the St Giles thoroughfare and then bear immediately right at the forked junction. Cross over St Giles into Banbury Road so that you are now on the right-hand side of St Giles Church and facing north. At the first set of traffic lights in Banbury Road turn right into Parks Road. As you approach the junction of Keble Road and Parks Road you will be able to look both ways to take in the enormity of the Keble College building! You will also notice as you progress throughout this tour that not all of Oxford's sixty famous college buildings and institutions within the University are the same size, shape or style. Remember it was Keble College where Jack met best friend and roommate Edward Courtenay Francis Moore, better known as 'Paddy' Moore. Paddy was the son of Mrs Janie King-Moore, who also had a daughter called Maureen, later to become Lady Dunbar.

Have You Made a Donation to the C. S. Lewis Foundation?

As I have no access to the C. S. Lewis Foundation accounts I can only guess at what the Foundation is doing with the funds raised but examples of their apparent 'lack of interest' in certain areas are plain for all to see. It is very upsetting for pilgrims who have travelled far, and often with a life-long ambition to be able to see inside, or even get close to the former home (which the C. S. Lewis Foundation owns), of the man who has changed their lives, then to be told, 'Sorry, viewing by appointment only.' It is a devastating blow for them, especially as the C. S. Lewis Foundation appear to do very little to encourage visitors or 'viewing by appointment' in the first place, with telephone calls and messages to the former home remaining unanswered. Emails similarly have been ignored. Some visitors who say they have previously made a donation believing they were helping to restore the property are furious beyond words, as they see the small gate at the tradesman's entrance, which has a sign attached to it that reads 'Private Residence, view by appointment'. Private residence? Isn't the property owned by a USA 501 (c) 3 Registered Charity?

So why aren't the telephone calls, messages etc. answered? Well, quite simply, the former home is occupied from September to June by international students. So how can they show anyone around? If you are ever lucky enough to get inside you will still only be shown five or six rooms because the students occupy the others as their home! Indeed, I have been confronted many times by some of the students who live at the Kilns, who have accused me personally, along with my guests on tour, of disrupting their studies with flash cameras, despite those photographs having been taken from the road, which is a public place, and despite the fact that I never carry a camera! For the record, we are never noisy and do not peer through windows as has been suggested. The students somehow think that they have a sole right to be there but forget all about their studies during the summer months when they can be seen having barbecues, sun-bathing and frolicking on the lawn! It is at times like this that they could have put their time to good use by showing visitors around the former home, thus helping with the finances of a property that looks as if it needs a little 'TLC' here and there!

During one rare occasion on 13th June 2004, I managed to gain 'entry to view' for a group of twenty-eight people from Atlanta, Georgia. During the five weeks of negotiations with the C. S. Lewis Foundation and at the Kilns with a student resident, I eventually received an email confirming their need for a donation, which was a recommended five pounds per person. The following paragraph is from that email, it reads:

> ...the Kilns is a private residence inhabited by students most of the year, not a museum, and because of this we receive very little funding for the upkeep and continual restoration of the Kilns.

That being the case, what is happening to the money given by well-meaning members of the public?

Anyway the internal viewing of the former Lewis home took place thus, one hundred and forty pounds for twenty-eight students and a thirty-minute tour! I offered them a hundred pounds on behalf of my visitors which was readily accepted. But now my question to the C. S. Lewis Foundation of Redlands, California, who presumably try to work to their mission statement is, what is happening to the money donated to the Foundation? Surely money is given by people who believe they are helping towards the renovation and restoration of the former home, among other things?

I requested a receipt for the hundred pounds, from the young lady that I was dealing with at the Kilns and was told, 'I don't have a till or a receipt pad.' I then asked for a receipt written on any piece of paper, toilet paper if needs be, the young lady huffed and puffed a little, but eventually handed me a receipt for the donation which I then passed to my visitors from Atlanta – I couldn't help but wonder if they had just contributed to a few bottles of wine, pork ribs and chicken wings for the celebration barbecue which was being set up on Sunday, 13th June 2004, just before the students returned home! With regard to the current use of the former Lewis home, my own view is that if international students want to study in Oxford then that is their prerogative but using the Kilns as a 'flop house', for want of a better description, is not acceptable. Further, the C. S. Lewis Foundation mission statement surely doesn't allow for casual friends and visitors of those students to visit, does it? Or, wait a minute, if it does then why can't they allow access to others on an 'ad hoc' basis rather than, as it seems, the select few? Why can't the students rent accommodation locally, after all they have been known to have employment in Oxford, which would free up the property for daily access to tourists? An entrance fee from each visitor would soon cover the mortgage, which can only be small compared to current market values. The house, in fact, is occupied throughout the year, or at least until the month of June, by the students, which I believe could be deliberate because, by coincidence, in July and August the C. S. Lewis Foundation then run six-day seminars' costing 2,695 dollars referred to on their website and held at the Kilns! What happens to all that money made in just two months? I can't help but wonder also if the whole issue of the Kilns described above could possibly be a very selfish but clever way of securing the Kilns as a 'holiday home' by a select few, who feel that they personally own the property. Could it be that the seminars that are held during the months of July and August are helping to keep it comparatively private and select and 'in line' with their mission statement and the charitable status which they enjoy! The fact remains that the

C. S. Lewis Foundation of Redlands, California, does not need the Kilns to conduct their business. In my opinion they are 'using' the Kilns as a snare to lure people to pay what I consider to be and what some of their fellow Americans think are their outrageously expensive seminar fees. These seminars could just as easily be conducted elsewhere.

My understanding is that the property referred to as the Kilns is owned by the C. S. Lewis Foundation, with a USA charitable status 501 (c) 3 Registration; as a result they have total control, not unreasonably so you might say. Surely, then, the minimal cost of cleaning Lewis' tombstone, for example, could come from the sum raised from the July/August seminars? Cost aside, I believe they have an obligation and a duty of care to keep it clean and tidy, thus engaging the services of a contractor at least on an annual basis. My opinion is that questions have to be asked over the Lewis tombstone because, as a result of the lack of attention it receives, it can only just about be seen in the churchyard of Holy Trinity and, further, there is a distinct lack of direction and/or identification, apart from a small plaque and an arrow pointing in the general direction, so unless you are accompanied by someone who knows the precise location, it is difficult to know where to start looking. Clearly more should be made of this very important tombstone, which, in my opinion, would not be out of place in Westminster Abbey! It is, to say the least, terribly disappointing to see the roots of the trees undermining the grave and the tall grass around the perimeter of the tombstone which, in turn, plays its part in making the granite slab very dirty. It makes it almost impossible to read the following lead-filled inscription. Some of the letters, in fact, are missing, but it reads:

In loving memory of
my brother
Clive Staples Lewis

born Belfast 29th November 1898
died in this parish
22nd November 1963

men must endure their going hence

Warren Hamilton Lewis
Major Royal Army Service Corps
born Belfast 16th June 1895
died in this parish
9th April 1973

So why is the humble tombstone of this so famous man dirty and in need of repair? I have previously been on my hands and knees scrubbing it and at my own expense but last year I decided not to do so any longer in view of the fact that the C. S. Lewis Foundation, who boast restoration and renovation, should surely bear the cost as well as the responsibility. Apart from any financial argument, it should be kept clean!

My personal thanks go out to those who took the trouble to complain, although in a letter from the C. S. Lewis Foundation dated 1st March 2001 I was told, 'That the graveyard and stones in question are maintained by Holy Trinity Church.' So that being the case, what does the C. S. Lewis Foundation do, what is its purpose? My suggestion would be that in the event it was not responsible for the cleaning, it should be!

Note: I believe the Americans who did the C. S. Lewis spring and summer tours with me did what they said they were going to do, this is complain to the C. S. Lewis Foundation about the state of the tombstone. Their complaints were obviously acted upon because the tombstone was cleaned on 17th May 2004.

The grave of the two Mrs Moore's in Holy Trinity churchyard is also in need of considerable work, which in view of the relationship to C. S. Lewis, should in my opinion also be cared for by the foundation.

Then there is Lewis' punt, which was recovered from the murky depths of the lake to the rear of the property during 1994. It happens that I was told during 1994 that the punt would be stored away in the attic of the house awaiting restoration one day. Well, they have had ten years so far, so how much more time do they want? I would suggest also that the timber will have dried out a long time ago and for that very reason has probably become nearly impossible to restore, but where is the punt today?

Back up at Lewis' former home the Kilns, some of the wooden window frames in the dormers around the property are very dirty and showing signs of substantial rot! So much so, that visitors on the C. S. Lewis Tour have photographed them, again fully intending to take the matter up with the C. S. Lewis Foundation when they return to America. Some have become visibly and verbally angry and have actually said, They'll get no more of our money. During August 2004, strips of white three-inch PVC angle appear to have been fitted to the bottom of some of the wooden window frames in various places to cover up the rotting timber behind, this is hardly restoration!

On 28th August 2004, Mr Stan Mattson, Founder and President of the C. S. Lewis Foundation of Redlands, California, invited me to a meeting at the Kilns. Also present was Mr Kym Gilnett, whom I met ten years ago, responsible then for the considerable restoration programme. We discussed many items during our meeting but still disagree on most. I put forward a case for an open house policy where all visitors can have access throughout the year and suggested that the National Trust become involved. Stan Mattson said the former home would never be open on a full-time basis and that they were looking at certain days of restricted opening hours, but access to the whole house would not be possible.

I also asked what happens to the money raised from internal viewings of the former home that have taken place previously. 'Over two thousand pounds was raised last year,' Stan Mattson said, he then added that the 'person who does the tour keeps half of the money.' For example, the young lady that did the tour for the Atlanta group on 13th June 2004 would have pocketed fifty pounds – that's not bad for thirty minutes of your time, especially if you have very little knowledge of Lewis, but you are staying at Lewis' former home, enjoying the 'intellectually and spiritually nourishing environment!' Further, bear in mind that the foundation is a Registered Charity and the 100 pounds was raised by showing a group around the former home. Wouldn't you think then that the full amount should have been handed over?

The students from Atlanta returned to their coach and immediately questioned me on the way the young lady kept saying 'I believe.' I believe C. S. Lewis this and that, I believe C. S. Lewis so and so, I believe C. S. Lewis something else, etc. Nothing positive, no facts! So why then should she have received payment? Perhaps the final insult comes from Stan Mattson and Kym Gilnett, who, when questioned, both confirmed that, 'She should not have done the tour, we were only trying to accommodate you.' Frankly, I would have preferred it if she had not been involved. I also enquired of the punt and was told by Kym Gilnett, 'I think we still have it but I don't know where it is.'

'The Foundation has no money' according to Stan Mattson, who also volunteered the information that they were 'eighteen thousand dollars in debt at the bank,' but in the next breath told me that 'they hoped to burn the mortgage this year.'

Stan Mattson has told me that the former Lewis home is not for sale, but I certainly hope to change his mind at some stage in the future because I find it very hard to accept that the property is owned by an American organisation, that appears not to want to open it up to the general public on a full-time basis. I passionately believe that it should be in the hands of the British people, it belongs to Britain as part of our Christian Heritage and I will continue to push to recover it.

No Plaque for C. S. Lewis

Most famous literary authors and their former homes are recognised with at least a plaque on the property, but when you arrive at Lewis Close, off Kiln Lane, there is absolutely nothing to even suggest that you are anywhere near this very important site that so many followers of Lewis want to see. No directions, no plaque, no recognition whatsoever. A typical example was an American visitor who did the C. S. Lewis Tour with me during May 2004 who said, as we drove through the streets of Headington Quarry 'I've been here before, I walked up and down here for half a day and still couldn't find the Kilns and nobody locally was able to help either, they just didn't know who or what I was talking about.' Sadly, that kind of statement is the norm.

The following articles and quotes were taken from the *Southern California Christian Examiner* (then called *Christian Times*) dated June 1997 and the *Oxford Mail* (1996), which were available on the internet at www.cslewis.org – the official webpage for the C. S. Lewis Foundation, so the information contained therein will be correct, won't it? You might be surprised.

Southern California Christian Examiner (then called the *Christian Times*), dated June 1997

According to an article published in the *Southern California Christian Examiner* then called *Christian Times* dated June 1997, Nicole

57

Coscarelli, then a student at the University of Redlands and an intern at the C. S. Lewis Foundation, wrote:

> The Foundation has no wish to create a shrine to C. S. Lewis, rather it intends to honour his memory by establishing an intellectually and spiritually nourishing environment that reflects something of Lewis' own lively Christian faith expressed through life of the mind and imaginative experience.

In my opinion the intellectually and spiritually nourishing environment referred to does not exist, rather I believe we have the 'flop house', meaning student accommodation aforementioned.

So far the C. S. Lewis Foundation has been able to keep its secret at the Kilns but with the release of the *The Chronicles of Narnia – The Lion, the Witch and the Wardrobe,* I suspect not for much longer! Apart from the paragraph quoted, there are some glaring mistakes contained within the article that should have been spotted long before its publication, especially considering the position of the writer. The full article was available on the internet at www.cslewis.org/news/ct.htm although today you will be redirected to www.cslewis.org/sitemap.html

Oxford Mail July 1996

In the *Oxford Mail,* dated 23rd July, Alan Carter wrote:

> Work to restore the Oxford home of C. S. Lewis is on target to be completed by the Centenary of the author's birth in two years, time... the project to renovate the house as a study centre for scholars and students is about two-thirds complete and should be finished by the 1998 Centenary...The Foundation says it is determined to maintain the special character of the house as a centre for contemplation and study, rather than

turning into a tourist attraction bringing in coach-loads of visitors.

Might I suggest you read that last paragraph again and ask yourself, so what is the Foundation all about and why do they need the former home as a place of study that could be pursued anywhere in the world?

In my opinion they are wrong and will ultimately pay the price for trying to 'keep it quiet'. The complete article was available on the internet at www.cslewis.org/news/oxfmail.htm

After reading another article published by a well-known American newspaper in August 1996, which was also once available at the Foundation's official website, frankly I wonder, having seen inside the former home over the last few years, just what house they were referring to. Perhaps I was blindfolded and taken elsewhere!

Various quotes make it clear what the Foundation intends to do with regard to the restoration. Stan Mattson refers to a place of contemplation for scholars, whilst admitting that making the house 'genuinely Lewisian' would be a challenge. However, he continues to encourage readers to believe that the details are of upmost importance and that no matter how small they will be dealt with by the volunteers, who even managed to produce something that looked like nicotine stains. Apparently, the projects mission was to reproduce the décor so that the rooms would appear to have been occupied by heavy smokers, which the Lewis brothers were of course.

So did they achieve their goal? I believe the simple answer is no, it does not look to me anything like it did in the 1950s, when it was cold and pretty dirty. But they have restored the property to a high standard internally making it a comfortable modern home for the international students that will inevitably arrive next year. For that reason access to some parts of the house will always be restricted whilst the Foundation continues to own the property.

Not a single piece of original furniture is on show in the former home, so don't get too excited about a photograph at Lewis' desk, if ever you do get inside!

The same article goes on to say that Jack and Warnie believed tobacco ash was good for keeping termites out of the carpet. The word 'termites' of course is an American expression and termites destroy buildings, furniture and household stores so when, or even if, Jack and Warnie ever said any such thing, they were probably referring to the theory that the tobacco ash would keep the 'moths' out of the carpets, which certainly was a generally held belief at the time.

Then a reference to the volunteers from America regarding the liberties they took whilst trying to make the house truly comfortable. One of those liberties it seems was excessive use of the vacuum cleaner, and the way I read it, it suggests they were cleaning up after the Lewis brothers, which of course is not the case, because the house was owned locally after the deaths of Jack and Warnie by a couple who put their own mark on it by replacing window frames, removing fireplaces and shelving etc. The house was later purchased by a group of businessmen in 1982, before the C. S. Lewis Foundation was offered it in 1993. So are they trying to convince us that a vacuum cleaner wasn't used in the house for over 20 years?

View by Appointment

Although the C. S. Lewis Foundation claim to accommodate visitors with a 'view by appointment' policy at the Kilns, which is painted onto a small plaque and attached to the gate; it is, in fact, very difficult to gain access to the former Lewis home unless you happen to be one of the wealthy who appear to lap up the July–August seminars. In fact, it seems the C. S. Lewis Foundation would rather you go on a walking tour, which they refer to as, Walking Guide of Lewis Oxford, for which they have then requested a five dollar donation in a recent email sent to a colleague, than have you visit the Kilns!

Download the information free of charge at www.cslewis.org/resources/walkguide.html At the bottom of the webpage they tell you that the guide doesn't mention Lewis' former home the Kilns, Holy Trinity Church, or the grave. I respectfully suggest that these are the very places that most want to see! However, for those who wish to attempt the near impossible the Head Resident at the Kilns can be contacted for further details on a direct dial telephone number (see p.11). Please do telephone. If you are lucky enough to arrange access there is currently no charge for entry, although they do expect a recommended donation, according to Founder and President Stan Mattson, of five pounds per person, up from three pounds last year! This, then, is probably where the young lady that I dealt with at the Kilns received her instructions with regard to the donation from my friends in Atlanta, Georgia. I have to say that paying five pounds per person would probably not deter anybody from viewing the former home. Indeed, they would just like the opportunity! As mentioned earlier there is no plaque and there are no directions to suggest who the house once belonged to, or where it is situated. Another attempt to dissuade you from getting anywhere near the place greets you on entering Lewis Close in Kiln Lane. You will see a sign attached below the official road sign which reads 'No Coaches'. This sign was erected by the local residents and is not legal, so take your vehicle up to Lewis' former home if you wish.

The only hint that you have found the Kilns at all is by way of a very small wooden sign which reads 'The Kilns' attached to the gable end of the property above the tradesman's entrance (the back door). This is where the post, bread and milk etc. would have been delivered, with the imposing brick kilns and brick-drying barn opposite. The old air-raid shelter that Fred Paxford built still exists in the woodland beyond the former Lewis home in the C. S. Lewis Reserve, which is owned by the Wildlife Trust, but is almost obliterated by undergrowth and brambles, which I suppose is how you would expect it to be. To find it you will have to have the resolve of 'Crocodile Dundee' but for those who wish to try, here are the directions. At the top of Lewis Close take the narrow muddy path walking towards the C. S. Lewis Henry Stephen Nature Reserve. Having entered the property through the small gate, turn immediately to your left. You will now be able to begin to fight your way through the woodland and brambles following the perimeter fence of the last property built in Lewis Close. At the furthest point (about fifty yards away) you will see the perimeter fence-line change direction, follow it to your right so that you now have a high bank to the front left of you. From here the entrance to the air-raid shelter is between you and the lake, hidden away under the bank, or as you face the lake about twenty yards away on the left.

The fact remains that to the average person the lake is still a disgrace, full of rubbish and fermenting weed, more about which you will read shortly! Many pilgrims must have got so close without actually realising that this particular property called the Kilns is, in fact, Lewis' former home – but it is only a very small part of the land that was once purchased and loved so by Mrs Janie King-Moore for the equal benefit of Jack and Warnie. With my vision of total restoration at the Kilns, I hope one day to be able to change the opinion of the C. S. Lewis Foundation thus allowing visitors access and bringing together once again this 'Land of Narnia' for the benefit of our future generations. You will read later of my ambitious plan to restore this site using the 'Lewis Awareness Fund', to be launched on the publication of this book.

Note: On 18th October 2004, whilst conducting a C. S. Lewis Tour, we met a group of people from the Wildlife Trust who were standing at the edge of the lake. I considered it an ideal opportunity to ask about the condition of the lake, the lack of fish and the amount of weed and general rubbish that gets thrown in. The person who appeared to be the leader of the group for the Wildlife Trust told me that the lake was environmentally in good condition. 'We now have dragonflies and damselflies in abundance' another member of the group added excitedly. I asked what had happened to all the fish and was promptly told that 'we don't want the fish they will eat the flies!' I then enquired about the air-raid shelter described previously. 'Why doesn't the Wildlife Trust open it up to the public?' I asked, 'after all it is part of the Lewis story.' The answer I got was, 'we have turned it into a home for bats, so it cannot be disturbed.' I am, to say the least, flabbergasted to think that flies and bats can be considered more important than C. S. Lewis, poet Shelley and or our history.

The Lake and Woodland

The once beautiful lake and surrounding woodland to the rear of the former home is, in my opinion, beautiful no longer. The freehold was acquired by the Berkshire, Buckinghamshire and Oxfordshire Naturalist Trust (BBONT) in 1969 but today is 'dubiously looked after' by the Wildlife Trust (they changed their name); who have the audacity to call it a nature reserve! Frankly, it is nothing more than an exercise yard for the local residents and their dogs. The muddy footpath leading to the lake is always fouled with dog faeces. The lake is surrounded by an assortment of trees that overhang in the most picturesque way that was once full of fish, such as roach, tench and perch, but today it is nothing short of a disgrace, a dumping ground for all sorts of rubbish, including a mix of bicycles, car seats, a wheelbarrow, metal frames, steel rope, bricks, stone, plastic drums, timber, bundles of newspapers still tied with a nylon band (which means the local paper boy/girl has dumped them rather than deliver them), and so much fermenting weed in the lake that there can be precious little oxygen left in the water to sustain any fish life. Red and white algae can be seen in the stagnant water at different times of the year and, of course, vandalism is rife! It is totally unacceptable for such an important and beautiful setting and one for which I believe a grant from the 'Heritage Lottery Fund' has been made available to the Wildlife Trust. Why, then, is it allowed to deteriorate at such an alarming rate? My opinion is that an enquiry into this environmental liability is surely long overdue.

Within my vision of total restoration at the Kilns I could accept that the Wildlife Trust may not wish to sell the lake and woodland because of the very nature of their activities, but we could still work together to bring the remaining greater percentage of the original plot, the former Lewis home and the surrounding eight houses that have been built on it to 'the Trust' in order to achieve the desired result – the reinstatement of the Kilns. The Wildlife Trust or the National Trust could then oversee a site that would be truly respected and visited by many thousands of people each year over many years to come. Quite simply, the houses that have been built on the former Lewis plot should be purchased as and when they become available, for later demolition. In the short term the properties could provide much needed rental accommodation with the proceeds being paid into the 'Lewis Awareness Fund'. That way, we would not be held to ransom by he who would wish to increase the price of the property, we just sit back and wait for them to become available. More details about this later.

The Original Entrance to the Kilns

The original entrance to the Kilns was a muddy lane off of Kiln Lane, Headington. It was no more than perhaps eight or nine feet in width and followed the line of an orchard right up to the house with a line of mature trees that still determine the original boundary. The sheep wire fencing was linked from tree to tree to keep the geese in and a wooden-fence typically six-foot-square panels on the right-hand side, would stop the neighbours from seeing into the property.

The orchard during the 1950s consisted of apple, pear and plum trees that had seen better days. They had not been pruned back as they should have been and so the fruit was small but plentiful and often diseased. The tall grass and stinging nettles underfoot were mown and the fruit-laden branches that inevitably fell to the ground under the weight allowed the geese their element. Imagine for a moment the awful noise from the bottom of the lane as visitors approached. The geese squawked and hissed relentlessly with their necks extended and their wings flapping furiously, as they followed the line of the fencing that separated them from he who dared to venture upon their territory!

There was an old garage at the top of the lane which has long been replaced with an extension to the original building, which now forms part of Lewis' former home. The gable end facing down Lewis Close (cul-de-sac), is where the two huge corrugated tin doors to the garage, which measured about eight feet square and hung on large 'T' hinges, creaked, squealed and groaned as they were opened. The garage is where Fred Paxford the gardener, spare cook and general handyman would keep his tools, lawn mowers, his bicycle etc. He would also store the fruit from the orchard in the garage which was then laid on a slatted shelving system just inside on the left. The shelving had previously been covered with old newspapers to stop the fruit falling through the wooden slats but there was no escaping the acid smell: a combination of the rotting fruit mixed with the petrol and oil that would inevitably spill as Fred mixed 'two stroke' for the lawn mowers! The smell wafted through the air permanently.

Generally speaking the garage was positioned in an ideal spot at the top of the lane for both parking access and location to the house. But, more importantly, the geese in the orchard at this point just yards away acted as an early warning system for Fred and whoever else may have been in residence. With Fred working in the garage he had a good view of what was going on and who was approaching. However, Fred hadn't reckoned with another school friend of mine, a crafty but loveable local lad who was nicknamed 'Crippin', who would bide his time watching and waiting in silence in the thick hedgerow at the bottom of the orchard bordering Kiln Lane, until a visitor arrived at the Kilns. As the visitor reached the top of the lane with the geese in hot pursuit Fred would come out of the house or garage to see what the fuss was about. In greeting the visitor he satisfied himself that all was well, but this was not always the case; sometimes, in fact, he was very wrong! Sometimes it provided the ideal opportunity and was the signal for Crippin to nip out of the hedgerow and into the orchard. He was intent on stealing the fruit from the orchard and the eggs from the geese and by doing so he would test Fred's agility to the limit. Fred was clearly no match for the nimble-footed Crippin, who managed to escape the clutches of Fred like a deer avoiding the hounds in the woodland! Fred never did catch him which was probably just as well really because in those day's summary justice would have been dealt out there and then in the orchard. Whilst Fred was generally a quiet sort who wandered about the Kilns whistling and humming to himself, he had a voice to shake the fruit from the trees, with fingers on the end of his hands that looked like a pack of thick pork sausages that had just been unwrapped!

After you have seen and photographed the former Lewis home, for which you should allow about '40 minutes' – restricting your viewing from the curb, taking care not to enter the grounds, according to Stan Mattson of the C. S. Lewis Foundation – follow the muddy footpath at the rear of the house and to the left of the house that appears to be in Lewis' back garden. Proceed through the gate at which the site you are entering is identified as a nature reserve – by now you will be facing the lake where it is believed the poet Shelley meditated and played with paper boats.

It is worth remembering that what you have now seen from the Kiln Lane entrance of Lewis Close, the land occupied now by the seven houses on the left-hand side, the house that appears to be in Lewis' back garden on the top right, and the lake with the woodland beyond, was once all part of the eight-acre plot called the Kilns!

The punt that Lewis owned was moored in the right-hand corner of the lake as you face it and although the length of the lake is not much more than seven or eight times the length of a punt and the breadth even less, one can imagine that Lewis would have been very happy to be idling away the occasional hour on water, perhaps even thinking about his next chapter.

Just opposite the tradesman's entrance of the former home were the aforementioned brick kilns and stone-walled brick-drying barn, where Dougie and I experimented with a bomb, the ingredients learned from schooldays. To the right of those buildings but camouflaged in the woodland was the air-raid shelter. The buildings were probably less than a hundred yards away from the house so that in the event of an air-raid warning during the war, the shelter was not too far to run. But overall what a fantastic place for us boys to play in and to explore. What must it have done for Janie King-Moore and the Lewis family? The peace and tranquillity is today only disturbed by the noise from the roads that surround it about a quarter of a mile away. Stand still at the lakeside and listen to the noise of the cars on the motorway; in Jack's day it really wasn't even as noisy as this!

To Continue with Directions

The Natural History Museum, a beautiful piece of architecture, is situated in Parks Road, almost opposite Keble College. About one hundred yards further down on the left, turn left at the traffic lights into South Parks Road, where you will see Rhodes House with the green dome-shaped roof on your right. (Ex-American President Bill Clinton became a Rhodes Scholar here.) As you proceed through what is known locally as the Science Area you are now in South Parks Road which as you bear right at the bottom of the road, with Linacre College now on the left, will take you into St Cross Road. Very soon you will be facing the thirteenth-century (some parts of the building are known to be earlier) Anglican St Cross Church, which is still in use today. In the St Cross Cemetery you will be able to find the graves of Inklings Hugo Dyson and Charles Williams. Kenneth Graeme, author of The Wind in the Willows is also buried there. As you pass St Cross Church now on your left, a short distance away also on the left in Longwall Street is the battlement-style perimeter wall of Magdalen College. At this stage, before you travel too far, you need to be looking across to the right between the buildings to see what remains of the old Oxford city wall, built in the year 1191. The first opportunity you get is as you follow the road bearing left at the end of St Cross Road into Longwall Street. (Holywell Street is now to your right. This is where J. R. R. Tolkien had 'digs' in 1916, with Mansfield Road, where C. S. Lewis lodged, also off to the right of Holywell Street.) A gap between the buildings on the right allows a quick glimpse of the city wall. The second opportunity is just fifty yards or so further into Longwall Street. However, during the month of May the leaf and apple blossom explodes into life on the trees in front of the old city wall making it impossible to see from Longwall Street until about late October time, so entry via New College in Holywell Street is where you will get your best photographs. New College is not part of the C. S. Lewis Tour route therefore a separate visit is recommended but there will be visitor restrictions at the College (Tel: +44 (0) 1865 279 555). Follow the Magdalen College battlement-style perimeter wall on the left looking out for the rear arched entrance to the College and you may be lucky enough to see part of the deer herd grazing within the three hundred acres of land owned by Magdalen College. You will shortly arrive at the end of Longwall Street where you need to turn left at the 'T' junction and traffic lights.

Magdalen College, The Great Tower, Magdalen Bridge and Addison's Walk

The building of Magdalen College began in 1458, although it was earlier called Magdalen Hall (1448), which was originally situated a few hundred yards nearer the city centre. The founder of Magdalen College was William of Wayneflete, then bishop of Winchester. During the thirteenth-century the site on which Magdalen College stands today was a hospital dedicated to St John the Baptist. However, it was in a state of disrepair and William of Wayneflete seized upon the opportunity, and obtained permission from Henry VI to build a new college. Building works started in 1458 which was, of course, Magdalen College, dedicated to St Mary Magdalen. The college has been made even more famous thanks to the film *Shadowlands*; a brilliant story about the life and love of C. S. Lewis, the family man. I have been asked many times if I considered the film true to life or fabrication. My answer has to be simply that this great film reflects upon the true love of C. S. Lewis and Joy Davidman because the producers were clever enough to know that it is how we, the public, would want to see it! No doubt some day we shall get another version which will add the events or details missing thus far.

Note: Towards the end of September – early October 2004 I was approached by a man who introduced himself as Norman Stone, who directed the original *Shadowlands* with Anthony Hopkins. We met outside the Eagle and Child public house in St Giles, Oxford, purely by chance, as the result of a parking meter not operating properly. He told me that he was about to make another film or drama/documentary about Lewis. A member of his team whom I have since met up at the Kilns whilst filming, had telephoned me previously collecting information about C. S. Lewis. I only have one thing to say to that...fantaaaaastic!

Jack also had rooms at Magdalen College, which were to be his home, one of several, for many years to come. Today those same rooms at the college are generally occupied and not open to the public for viewing. My personal view is that the College could afford the public the opportunity to see them whilst generating a source of income.

Ten minutes for photographs from outside Magdalen College is considered sufficient time here because the biggest problem you will encounter if you are driving is managing to evade the dreaded traffic wardens! The double yellow lines on the road means that vehicles must not stop at any time, so it is quite useful to have a local driver who is prepared to 'risk it' while you take your photographs. There are also restricted hours of entry that apply to Magdalen College in the event that you wish to take in 'Addison's Walk', named after a journalist and Fellow of Magdalen College, Richard Addison, who remained at the College for some twenty years. The water meadows are not part of the C. S. Lewis Tour route, therefore separate arrangements need to be made. The walk follows the edge of the meadow with an assortment of wild flowers and birds to make you 'wow' with excitement, bearing in mind that you are still in the centre of Oxford city. If you do walk the meadow, about half-way round you will see a plaque with a poem inscribed upon it, which was written by Lewis, called *What the Bird Said Early in the Year*.
It reads as follows:

> I heard in Addison's walk a bird sing clear
> This year the summer will come true this year, this year
> Winds will not strip the blossom from the apple trees
> this year, nor want of rain destroy the peas
> This year time's nature will no more defeat you
> nor all its promised moments in their passing cheat you
> This time they will not lead you round and back

to Autumn one year older by the well worn track
This year, this year, as all these flowers foretell
we shall escape the circle and undo the spell
Often deceived yet open once again your heart
quick, quick, quick, quick, the gates are drawn apart.

(Poems by C. S. Lewis copyright© C. S. Lewis Pte. Ltd. Reprinted by permission.)

Magdalen Bridge, High Street, Oxford, was constructed during the years 1772–8. The bridge is famous for the May Day celebrations that take place, during which up to twelve thousand people will congregate on the morning of 1st May to await the Magdalen College choir. At 6am precisely there is a silence that will amaze you. The choir will then perform the traditional *hymnus eucharisticus,* as in the film *Shadowlands,* from the top of Magdalen College Great Tower to the crowd below; it was composed in the late eighteenth century by a former Fellow of Magdalen College during term. (The Magdalen College choir also sings evensong six evenings a week at 6pm.) The Great Tower was built between 1490 and 1510 and stands at an amazing 150 feet in height!

Soon after the 'May morning' event is over the ladies in their evening gowns and the men in their 'penguin' suits can be seen hurrying and sometimes staggering away from the bridge area to sleep off the hangover which must surely follow. Students and locals alike are quite often under the influence of alcohol having celebrated throughout the previous evening.

The purpose of the festivities on May morning is to welcome in the sunrise and from past personal knowledge scenes of riotous behaviour and jubilation could well end up with somebody trying to jump from the bridge parapet into the River Cherwell below, sadly only to end up in the local hospital because, first, there is about a ten-metre drop and, second, the depth of the water, which is dependent on rainfall, of course, is only two to four feet at this point! The water can at best be described as 'dirty' so goodness knows what else you might be the owner of by the time you are fished out! There were thirty injuries during the 2005 celebrations.

Before you proceed over Magdalen Bridge may I suggest you cross over to the other side of the road, being aware of the traffic flow of course, to take a few photographs of the Magdalen College Great Tower which apparently sways as the bells peel because it was built on minimal foundations, and the local area, which will provide you with some memorable shots. You may even be lucky enough to get a photograph of the College courtyard from the High Street or a shot from inside the College grounds by walking about two hundred yards back towards Oxford city and speaking with the porters at the Lodge.

Magdalen College is open to the public during the following periods: 1st April–30th June, 1pm until 6pm; 1st July–30th September, 12 noon until 6pm; and 1st October–31st March, 1pm until dusk (Tel: +44 (0) 1865 276 030. The charge for adults is three pounds per person, senior citizens and students two pounds per person, which allows access to various parts of the College, including Addison's Walk where Lewis, Tolkien and Dyson had many a conversation about Christianity.

To cope with the weight imposed upon it during the May Day celebrations Magdalen Bridge has been strengthened recently, although the actual numbers allowed onto the bridge for the occasion are now restricted to eight or nine thousand at any one time. During May 2004, Oxford City Council employed private security officers to keep the remaining three or four thousand people on either side of the barriers erected for the occasion. The bridge is now included as one of Oxford's alcohol-free zones so the bottles of champagne, wine, spirits etc. and cans of beer that inevitably arrive with the students have been banned and therefore will be confiscated before they reach the bridge. But by sunrise it doesn't matter too much anyway because the alcohol has already been consumed in many of the College bars in the City that will have been serving late, or perhaps even early!!

Punting on the River Cherwell and the May Day Festivities

Punts on the Cherwell can be seen throughout most of the year moored in the location of Magdalen Bridge. They can be hired out from a local company called Salters Steamers Ltd, Folly Bridge, Abingdon Road, Oxford. Salters Steamers Ltd can be contacted on +44 (0) 1865 243 421. The punts can be hired from April until October 10am–6pm, and the current charge is ten pounds per hour. I have to say that nothing quite beats the leisurely summer activity of 'punting'; the girls and the punnets of strawberries, boaters and of course the champagne, provided that is, you are not the unfortunate individual that is elected to make it move!

The Plain and Magdalen College School

Photo session over on the bridge, you are now approaching an area known locally as 'The Plain'. Look for the fourth exit at the round-about, which will take you into Cowley Place and you will be able to see Magdalen College School on the left. Magdalen College School, Oxford, which was founded in 1480, has many famous 'old boys' names to its credit, such as St Thomas More, Cardinal Wolsey, William Campden, Thomas Hobbes, Ivor Novello and Basil Blackwell. Two recently successful old boys include Sam Mendes, awarded an Oscar for *American Beauty,* and Tim Hunt, who received a Nobel Prize for medicine.

Magdalen College School is one of England's leading academic schools, providing education for over six hundred boys from the age of seven to eighteen years, many of whom then go on to degree courses at Oxford and Cambridge universities. C. S. Lewis is believed to have paid into a scholarship fund for some of the pupils to attend over the years, with money earned from his writing and broad-casting.

My friend and playmate Douglas Gresham, one of the two step-sons of Lewis, attended Magdalen College School during the mid-1950s for a while and it was Dougie that I would look forward to meeting, after school was over, to play at the Kilns, as schoolboys did in those days, swapping stamps, coins, cigarette cards, shooting, fishing, bomb making...yes bomb making, about which I shall explain later.

St Hilda's College

St Hilda's College, opposite Magdalen College School, was founded in 1893 by Dorothea Beale, who was Principal of Cheltenham Ladies, College; five of its first students had been her pupils. In 1897, St Hilda's became a hall. For the next thirty years or so a strong link existed between the Hall and Cheltenham but this was broken in 1926, when the hall was granted the right to be governed by an independent Oxford-based Council and became St Hilda's College. In 1955, the Council was replaced by a governing body consisting of the Principal and the Fellows of the College. The Principal, Fellows and students, both undergraduates and graduate students, are all women.

The original house, bought by Dorothea Beale, is now the centre of the Old Hall building; it was constructed for Professor Humphrey Sibthorpe at the end of the eighteenth century and extended by Sir Benjamin Birdie in the 1860s. Dorothea Beale added more student rooms in 1897 and a further wing was built in 1909 with money left by her at her death.

In 1920, the number of students was substantially increased to a hundred when South Building was acquired; this building had formerly been a training college and prior to that it had been a large family house built for Augustus Vernon Harcourt in 1878. More students rooms and a library were added to Hall Building in 1935. After the Second World War, the buildings of Milham Ford Girls' School, which had separated Hall and South buildings, became part of the College to add yet more residential accommodation with the

Sacher Wing, Wolfson and the Garden Buildings. The most recent additions are the Jacqueline du Pre Music Building (1995) and the Christina Barratt Building (2001).

Amongst the nine principals, two were former students of St Hilda's; the first principal was Mrs Esther Burrows and the present principal, Lady English, has held office since 2001. The many distinguished graduates of the College include writers, scholars, journalists and members of a wide range of professions. Authors D. K. Broster, Dame Helen Gardner, Barbara Pym, Angela Lambert, Val McDermid and poets Jenny Joseph and Wendy Cope were all students of St Hilda's. C. S. Lewis was also tutor for many of St Hilda's students reading English, who remember their time there as 'golden' and who talk with great respect and fondness of him, along with Lord David Cecil.

The Ampleforth Arms and the Empty Cider Bottles

As young lads Dougie and I also fetched the beer from the local public house called the Ampleforth Arms (the Amp). Who was the beer for? Well, it wasn't for Dougie or I and there was normally only Warnie or Fred at the Kilns and Fred would cycle to the pub! That said, Dougie did sample the beer, I remember he was partial to a cigarette, as well as a drink from what I thought at the time was a smelly discoloured tin mug – it was, of course, a pewter mug which I had not previously seen, but was typical of beer tankards at the time. All this was well before his sixteenth birthday!

I believe the landlord of the Ampleforth Arms at the time was a man called Mr Markham. Then, a packet of Smiths Crisps cost 3d (three old pennies) and contained a little blue wrapper of salt twisted into a pineapple shape. Dougie and I would be given the two empty cider bottles up at the Kilns and told to fetch the beer. We would wander down to the off-licence, which was the part of the public house where children were allowed to buy sweets, crisps ('chips'), chocolates etc. We could just about reach up to the high counter, handing over the bottles to whoever was serving but they knew who the beer was for! The bottles would be taken through to the bar room pumps at the back of the pub, re-filled with beer and then returned to us at the off-licence counter. The froth from the beer still spilling down the outside of the bottles would be wiped away before we then paid for them and returned to the Kilns.

J. R. R. Tolkien's Former Home in Sandfield Road

To continue, with Magdalen College School and St Hilda's College now behind you, come out of Cowley Place, taking the second exit at the roundabout towards Headington which effectively means that from where you are in Cowley Place you need to be heading for the right-hand corner of the roundabout. Continue through 'St Clements' and up Headington Hill, at the top of which you will see an entrance to Oxford Brookes University, Headington Campus, on the left hand side. Oxford Brookes University, known locally as just 'Brookes', also have another establishment on your right about two hundred yards away, as well as several others throughout Oxfordshire. You are now travelling along Headington Road. Continue on this road for about five hundred yards, passing traffic lights, and on your left a road called Headley Way. A public house called the 'White Horse' is also on the left at this junction. Continue for another three hundred yards and then turn left into Sandfield Road.

Inkling Henry Victor 'Hugo' Dyson (1896–1975)

Henry Victor 'Hugo' Dyson, a member of the Inklings and former lecturer and tutor at Oxford and Reading Universities, lived at 32 Sandfield Road, Headington, Oxford, until 1975 (drive-by only).

This property has undergone substantial private renovation recently and is not, therefore, as it would have been during the 1950s. Look for 76 Sandfield Road, about six hundred yards further down on the left-hand side also, where another Inkling, namely J. R. R. Tolkien, lived with his wife Edith from 1953–68.

Inkling John Ronald Reuel Tolkien (1892–1973)

Today the name John Ronald Reuel Tolkien is known the world over and is part of most people's vocabulary. He will certainly be known by the younger generation, whereas if you asked them who C. S. Lewis was you would be met with a silence and blank stare. Things will surely change after the release of *The Chronicles of Narnia – The Lion, the Witch and the Wardrobe,* which I am told is being co-produced by Douglas Gresham in New Zealand currently, and is due to hit the screens in December 2005…can't wait!

As you face Tolkien's former home at 76 Sandfield Road, look to the left of the property and you will see a stone tablet above the garage, that Tolkien used to use as a library and where I am told he finished *The Lord of the Rings,* recording the dates. In those days the garage was single storey. The property is owned privately today but the residents are aware of the importance of this site and have been very co-operative and understanding, for which I now publicly thank them. A quiet photograph standing on Tolkien's former driveway is surely a must after the recent success of *Lord of the Rings,* for which I am told he sold the rights to the story for a hundred thousand pounds, believing that nothing could be done with it! I wonder what Tolkien or his wife Edith who, according to the neighbours, were 'lovely people' would think of the recent success and the vast sums of money made?

Generally, these properties in Sandfield Road are as they were during the Tolkien days, with possibly the double-glazed windows and the odd extension (the property has been made bigger) here and there being the only difference. So as you see the area today Tolkien would have seen it during the time he spent there, perhaps as he walked to Headington or the Kilns, the flowering cherry or horse chestnut trees in particular making a real impression against the well-maintained houses in the summer sunshine. During the years 1930–47 Tolkien lived at 20 Northmoor Road, Oxford, which is to the north of Oxford city, off of the Banbury Road and which would have been nearer to the Eagle and Child for the Inkling's meetings that took place. This former home is not included in the C. S. Lewis Tour so you will need to make your own arrangements to view but if you are in Oxford city you are only ten minutes away!

After the photographs at Sandfield Road, you need to turn round and go back to the 'T' junction that has now become the London Road (Headington Road merges with London Road). At the 'T' junction turn left and follow the London Road for about six hundred yards until you reach the traffic lights with Old High Street, now on your left.

The former home of Helen Joy Davidman.

Having turned left at the traffic lights, 10 Old High Street, Headington, is about two hundred yards away on the left. This property is for sale as I write, with a guide price tag of three hundred and fifty thousand pounds upon it, which may seem a lot of money for what you get in material terms, but I feel strongly that it should be preserved along with all other Lewis 'connected properties' for future generations. The property was, however, the former home of Joy Gresham (née Davidman), an American Jewess, poetess and authoress perhaps best known for a book called *Smoke in the Mountain.* Joy was married to William Gresham in 1942. Their two sons, namely Douglas and David Gresham, would later become the step-sons of C. S. Lewis.

Joy Gresham had been corresponding with Lewis since 1950 and had had several meetings with him in Oxford from September until December 1952. Joy Gresham left America for England and in 1953 she took up residence in London and then 10 Old High Street, Headington, where it seems likely that Jack's offer of help at the time was itself a hint of what was to come. However, it was whilst she was here that she received a letter from her husband William Gresham, who was still in America, a letter that was to signal the beginning of the end of their marriage.

As you face 10 Old High Street a stone tablet confirms that writer Joy Davidman, wife of C. S. Lewis, lived here. One wonders if whoever was responsible for this memorial plaque knew that Joy's full name was Helen Joy Davidman, even though she liked to be called Joy. This stone tablet also happens to be one of only two memorials that I know declaring that Joy Davidman was the wife of author C. S. Lewis, the other stone tablet memorial being the plaque in cloister two in the Garden of Remembrance at Oxford Crematorium. Another good reason, then, to set up the Lewis Awareness Fund, which could fund an appropriate memorial to Jack and Joy. It would enable us to erect a memorial to this husband and wife team, Mr and Mrs C. S. Lewis, a couple who have gone down in history but who are never referred to as such. I believe the memorial should be erected in a place where pilgrims could just sit and be quiet for a while, wondering perhaps what might have been had they not been taken from us so prematurely. My thoughts are that neither Jack nor Joy would have wanted a fuss to be made, but modern day feelings suggest to me that we must do something to promote the work of this unique couple. What better way than to start with a memorial, which would inspire the public to ask, 'Who were they?'

The NOC main entrance (formerly the Wingfield Hospital) and the Mayfair Suite

Having taken your photographs of Joy's former home, go back to the traffic lights and cross over into Windmill Road. Follow the road for about six hundred yards; down on the bottom right is the hospital, today called the Nuffield Orthopaedic Centre known locally as the 'NOC' but formerly known as the Wingfield Hospital. This is also the hospital that Douglas Gresham refers to in a book that he wrote called *Lenten Lands*, where he recalls his memories after walking through the main entrance of the hospital, where Jack told him that he was taking him to see his mother who had a broken leg. In fact, this was the hospital where, in December 1956 in a private ward called the Mayfair Suite, Jack and Joy's marriage was blessed in a bedside ceremony that was performed in accordance with the rites of the Church of England because Joy's death from cancer was thought to be imminent.

During 1957 Joy was said to have made a remarkable recovery, today I suppose we would say that she was in remission. The recovery was such that in July 1958 Jack and Joy went on holiday together to Ireland and even managed later to travel to Greece. They returned from Greece in April 1960 and Joy died three months later in July 1960 at the Radcliffe Infirmary, Woodstock Road, Oxford. Mrs C. S. Lewis was just forty-five years old.

The construction of a new hospital at the Nuffield Orthopaedic Centre is well under way during May 2004, which suggests that the 'NOC' or some of the original Wingfield Hospital buildings could well be demolished by 2006, the expected completion date, so get those photographs on tour before it's too late! (Data Protection Act – be careful not to include members of the public in your photographs).

After you have seen the Nuffield Orthopaedic Centre and perhaps photographed the main entrance to the hospital and the Mayfair Suite, which is towards the rear of the old hospital, turn round and leave the hospital via the Windmill Road exit, where you came in. As you approach Windmill Road turn right and continue for about three hundred yards before turning second left into Old Road. Follow the road for about five hundred yards and turn second left into Quarry Road, staying on this road for about five hundred yards, and then turn right into Quarry Hollow. As you get to the bottom of Quarry Hollow about one hundred yards away turn right into Quarry School Place, which is a very narrow and twisting 'S' bend with an immediate steep rise bearing right.

Quarry Hollow(drive by enroute)
The Masons Arms public house and
Holy Trinity Church

The Masons Arms

The stone used to build Holy Trinity Church was literally dug out of Quarry Farm Pit which was behind the Masons Arms public house and carried across the road to the piece of land on which Holy Trinity Church stands today. The Masons was another watering hole frequently used by Jack and Warnie and a photograph of this quaint old English pub built in 1872, is surely a must. Today the pub, is a 'free house' owned by the Meeson family. The current owners will be pleased to serve you beers and real ales with, no doubt, their memories of the Lewis brothers. Opening hours for the Masons Arms are as follows: Monday 7pm-11pm, Tuesday to Friday 5pm-11pm, Saturday 12 noon-11pm, Sunday 12 noon- 4pm, and then again 7pm-10.30pm. I also happen to believe that the Masons Arms could be the answer to the mystery as to why Jack and Warnie always left church early, which you will find out about a little later.

Holy Trinity Church

On 9th June 1847 a sermon that was preached by Bishop Wilberforce in St Aldate's Church, Oxford, urged the need for a church in the 'hamlet' called Headington Quarry. The assistance of our Christian neighbours was sought and successful appeals for money allowed the building work to commence in Headington

Quarry on 19th June 1848. The foundation stone, which is believed to be below ground, was laid by Bishop Wilberforce. Seventeen months later and at a cost of three thousand pounds, which was raised by voluntary effort, the building work was completed. The church came into being when it was consecrated by Bishop Wilberforce on 22nd November 1849.

When you reach Holy Trinity Church probably the first thing that you will notice as you walk through the heavy oak doors, apart from its own natural beauty, is the musty and old wood smell that somehow grips you with an instant 'This is Lewis!' In fact, I can tell you that the smell permeating from the old wooden pews, the stone and quarry tiles is not at all offensive and probably what you would actually expect it to be within the church. However, the point is I remember it smelling exactly the same as a ten-year-old lad as I attended church with my parents and other family members. In other words, it hasn't changed since the days when the Lewis brothers worshipped here, so enjoy it!

Although currently there are no premises in Oxford selling specifically 'Lewis memorabilia,' there is a small collection of merchandise including such items as postcards, tea towels, mugs, key fobs, thimbles, trinket boxes, milk jugs etc. available at the rear of the church, the proceeds of which go towards the upkeep of the building. Payment and offerings should be deposited in the wall safe to the left-hand side of the door as you leave. You are also invited to record your visit by signing the visitors' book.

Holy Trinity or Quarry Church in Headington Quarry as it is known locally is where the Lewis brothers Jack and Warnie worshipped regularly. In fact they were members of the church congregation for over thirty years! Today you can visit the Lewis brothers' grave in the churchyard of Holy Trinity, where Warnie was buried in the same grave beside his brother Clive Staples Lewis in 1973.

Once inside the church take a few moments to study the beauty of the stained glass east window above the altar that was inserted in 1951 as a memorial to those of the parish who died in the Second World War. It was designed by Sir J. Ninian Comper, whose mark (a strawberry) can be seen in the bottom right hand corner. The window depicts Christ in Glory. The insignia at the top is that of Holy Trinity and the two lower trefoils contain the crests of Lord Nuffield and the Diocese of Oxford.

The Rev. A. Dalton, vicar of the parish from 1867–70 had placed the first piece of stained glass in the church in this window, the centrepiece of which (a Gothic crucifixion) was later installed in the Lady Chapel. The stained glass window by the pulpit was installed in 1910 in memory of the Rev. P. Longland (vicar, 1870–91) and his daughter Mary Elizabeth, who died at the age of fourteen years. The picture is of an angel who holds the text from St John, 'God so loved the world that he gave his only begotten son.' The text was the title of a book of sermons preached in Holy Trinity by the Rev. P. Longland and published in 1897. The Baptistry window depicts the descent of the Holy Ghost on the font (showing the font of Holy Trinity Church) together with the virgin and child. The window dates from 1916 and is a memorial to Kate Johnston, wife of Charles Johnston (vicar, 1891–1916). The windows in the Chancel depict St Andrew (patron saint of the parish) and Saint Philip. They were installed in memory of the Rev. Philip Doyne (vicar, 1916–24). The windows were incorrectly assembled in the workshop and each saint has the gospel scene belonging to the other!

The Lewis Pew, Narnia window and Holy Trinity churchyard

You will also be able to see exactly where the Lewis brothers sat. A small brass plaque records what has become known as the Lewis 'pew' and just opposite is the spectacular Narnia window installed in 1991. Lewis' first ever sermon was preached in the University Church of St Mary the Virgin, on 22nd October 1939, soon after the start of the Second World War. The idea of writing *The Screwtape Letters* came to him following an 8am Communion service at Holy Trinity Church. He first preached at Holy Trinity at evensong on 29th March 1942, his subject being religion and pleasure. In 1943 he preached on 'Forgiveness' and in 1944 on 'Miracles'. There were a number of further addresses in the years that followed. At this time he was becoming famous outside Oxford, largely as a result of his publications, *The Problem of Pain* (1940) and his broadcasts on BBC Radio on *What Christians Believe.* These talks, delivered with the clarity and focus drawn from his years of doubt, caused immense interest and drew many others to Christianity.

Although Lewis earned money from his talks it is known that he gave most of his earnings away to worthy causes and individuals who needed help. His own surroundings at work and at home remained fairly austere.

1950 saw the publication of his first *Chronicle of Narnia The Lion, the Witch and the Wardrobe,* and established him as one of the most original writers of his day. Now regarded as classic children's literature, the Narnia books have also drawn children to understand the Christian interpretation of death and resurrection through their allegorical stories.

The Narnia Window and the Howe Bequest

As previously mentioned, just opposite the Lewis pew, you will see the Narnia window, paid for by the Howe bequest. The window is a memorial to the Howe family, George and Kathleen and their two children, who also worshipped regularly in Quarry Church. Sadly George and Kathleen Howe lost their two children, at the early age of just two years and sixteen years; their son William sang in the choir.

The Howe estate was divided between Holy Trinity Church and Lord Williams School, situated about ten miles away in a village called Thame, Oxfordshire, where William was a pupil when he died. Through the Howe bequest Holy Trinity Church was asked to install a stained glass window in the church as a memorial and was given a free choice as to its subject. It seemed in order, then, that the bequest should be spent on what would be an appropriate choice of theme as a memorial not only to the Howe children but to all other children and adults alike throughout the world. Hence the Narnia window, a spectacular piece of work installed alongside the pew where Jack and Warnie habitually sat and, since Lewis lived in the parish, it is very appropriate that his contribution to classic children's literature should also be commemorated in this place. This remarkable engraved glass window depicts Aslan the lion shown as a sun. This also emphasises his role in the story as a Christ-like figure radiating light and life. The word Narnia appears amongst the rays of light coming from his mane which emphasises his role as life-giver to Narnia. The waterfall spanning the two main panes descends from his paw to show how he brings about the creation of Narnia. Also depicted are the Castle Cair Paravel, fledge, the flying horse, the magic apple tree on the left panel and a talking tree on the right panel with many of the other animals who feature in the stories. The gifts given to the children of Narnia are placed on a ledge at the bottom of the window; the medicine bottle, sword and shield, bow and arrow with the horn above as we look past them into the land of Narnia. I have heard many a visitor comment over the detail in the Narnia window. They will study it closely with the inevitable 'Oh, wow', followed by 'Look, they have even got the medicine bottle in it, look the bow and arrow, the lantern etc.'

The love of C. S. Lewis and the tears that frequently flow as pilgrims sit quietly in the Lewis pew is a special and very powerful experience, while they continue to be overwhelmed by the beauty of both the church and the Narnia window, which was engraved by Sally Scott and installed in the church in the north aisle on 2nd July 1991. Very often pilgrims have told me that they have felt the closeness of Lewis in the church, and that the tour has completed a part of their lives that they have longed for. Who am I to argue with that?

The Lewis Brothers' Grave/Tombstone

As you leave Holy Trinity Church follow the narrow churchyard path for about twenty-five yards, passing on the right the churchyard cross, a memorial to those of the parish who died in the 1914–18 War and whose names are inscribed on a stone tablet in the church porch. You will shortly see in front of you a sign that reads 'C. S. Lewis' grave', which is secured to the stone wall and directing you to the tombstone. The Lewis tombstone, is the sixth one along under the tall pine trees about fifteen yards away on the left-hand side.

In the churchyard brothers Jack and Warnie are buried side by side. Their grave can be seen under these towering pine trees with an ivy plant clinging to the trunk of the tree nearest to the tombstone. The leaf of the ivy is a rich dark green, the new growth being paler in colour, proclaiming new life as the sunshine bursts through the trees. I wonder whether you are one of the lucky pilgrims who have already completed the C. S. Lewis Tour. If so, did you accept an ivy leaf from the plant that clings to the pine tree alongside Lewis' tombstone as an additional 'memento' to the personalised certificate that I issue after the tour is over? If so, here is the official confirmation that the ivy plant really does exist!

The humble Lewis tombstone soon has you wondering why there is not more of an appropriate memorial to this most famous, even notorious, man. Further, there is no mention of Joy Davidman (Joy's body was cremated at Oxford Crematorium two miles away and her ashes scattered) and my personal view is that there should be. A brass plaque perhaps could be secured beneath the Lewis brother's inscription, for which there is plenty of room. I also believe they deserve an appropriate memorial, possibly somewhere in Oxford city, and maybe within the grounds of Magdalen College or one of Oxford's parks because of Lewis's life-long connections with the College and Oxford University. In this way we could at last bring this now so popular husband and wife team together in name at least, in order that pilgrims from afar can sit and reflect on what might have been and where the local community can at last begin to understand the importance of who C. S. Lewis and Joy Davidman were.

The Rev. Tom Honey has been Priest-in-charge at Quarry Church since 1995. Rev. Tom Honey is keen to allow visitors into his church but obviously commitments on any particular day will determine whether or not that is possible. Tom, as he has become known to me has allowed me a set of keys to the church and I will show you round, commitments permitting of course, if you decide to take a guided C. S. Lewis Tour. Other than this, the church is open periodically for visitors.

The Lewis brothers, Clive Staples (Jack) and Warren Hamilton (Warnie), worshipped at Holy Trinity Church for over thirty years. Brother Warnie was Churchwarden at Holy Trinity Church from 1953–7. If you get the opportunity to sit in the pew where Jack and Warnie sat then I think you will agree that they had a good view of the Pulpit yet were sufficiently screened from the rest of the congregation. They usually arrived early but left just before the end of each service with few people noticing, except, that is, on the occasions when they dropped a walking stick, for example. They were described as 'strangely clumsy with their hands' by the Rev. Canon R. E. Head, Vicar of Holy Trinity Church (1956–90) who also recorded a tape about the brothers titled, *Two People of the Foothills,* the transcript of which has been copied and reprinted in this guide by kind permission of the Rev. Tom Honey of Holy Trinity Church, Headington, Oxford. In Lewis' book *Surprised by Joy* he refers to a physical defect that both he and Warnie inherited from their father. They each only had one joint in their thumbs, the top joint appearing normal but in fact they were unable to bend it, so this may account for their clumsiness.

I would like to take this opportunity to publicly thank the Rev. Tom Honey for his valuable contribution to this guide and in particular his patience after I have approached him many times in the churchyard with pilgrims from afar who were thrilled to be introduced to him personally. So Tom, my sincere thanks, you thoroughly deserve this piece of history in the beautiful Holy Trinity Church.

Nobody really knows the reason for Jack and Warnie's early departure from Holy Trinity Church but as you have read earlier I believe the Masons Arms could have played a major role, quite simply they wanted to be first at the bar for a beer!

However, when they did leave, recalls Rev. Head, 'they could not quite manage the bogus medieval door latch' (maybe those thumbs again!). The Lewis brothers often had so much difficulty with the door latch that he asked the Verger be on hand as the brothers left church to open the door for them. Strangely many visitors that I have taken to Holy Trinity Church on tour have experienced similar difficulty, although they, unlike the Lewis brothers, haven't had over thirty years to get used to it! The Verger is a luxury no longer afforded today but is someone, a church official, who takes care of the interior of the church and who acts as an attendant.

Transcription of a tape – *Two People of the Foothills*

The Rev. Canon R. E. Head, Vicar of Holy Trinity Church, Headington Quarry (1956–90), Curate (1952–6), recorded the following in Holy Trinity Church, Headington Quarry, Oxford, England (7th July 1988).

I suppose in welcoming you, I should first of all say something about the church in which you are actually sitting. It's always useful I suppose to start with that. Although, of course, it's a building of antique appearance constructed in the fifteenth-century style, it's a place which was built quite recently – not having arrived on the scene until 1849. It is, however, quite a good immitation of a medieval church – one, which was built originally with a Sanctuary and a Nave and then, of course, the idea being the aisle was added on afterwards. They always look as if it was added on afterwards, which is quite a feat on the part of the builders. In Oxford, of course, buildings are only old if they were, in fact, erected here before the Norman Conquest and even, after all, you will know that William of Wykeham's College of St Mary of Winchester, founded in 1379, bears the significant title of 'new'. Very few of our people know what its actual title was. If you said you were going to the College of St Mary of Winchester – they look at you blankly – never heard of the place, but it is New College.

Now this Church itself remains substantially unaltered from the day it was built except that originally the roof had plaster in between the rafters, which would, of course, give a totally different appearance and would, of course, in those days have made it much warmer. Unfortunately, the plaster fell down in 1912, narrowly missed the Vicar, apparently, when he was kneeling here, and the result was that it was all taken down and the whole thing boarded in so that you see it as it is today. They didn't have heating until 1870. In those days, as in the Middle Ages, they wrapped themselves up in many clothes and sat there in the cold. The organ itself arrived here in 1912.

The church, dedicated to the Holy Trinity, is correctly orientated so the sun actually rises directly behind the eastern window on the 22nd day of November, being the day of the church's consecration. The eastern window, designed by Comper, with his little strawberry mark in the right-hand corner at the bottom there, is, of course, Christ in Glory, eternally youthful. This was an idea of which Comper was very fond, and is in sort of Byzantine Medieval style, rather looking like a seal or an ornamental capital in a manuscript. It replaced the Gothic crucifixion, which was originally put here in 1867 and which now stands in the frame at the bottom of the aisle at the western end. At this end, the eastern end of the aisle, you can see the screen which is surmounted by a copy of a French fifteenth-century Gothic virgin and child, the original of which is kept in the Victoria and Albert Museum. At the western end of the church, the Baptistry window (in the corner there), portrays the descent of the

Holy Ghost on the font, together with Our Lady and the Holy Child and the font (which you'll have to look at afterwards), is actually a picture of the real font, which is there.

The list of vicars on the board behind the font, reveals all sorts of interesting things about the place and about their various degrees of stamina in actually remaining here. It's not, of course, an old English custom to keep the weathervane by the font. If, however, you've never seen a weathervane really close up, today is an opportunity to do so! The Cockcrow of the Passion is, of course, the significance of having a cock on the weathervane and I hope that, of course, the whole apparatus will soon be returned to its rightful place above the crumbling Bellcote tower from which it was blown down about two years ago. Indeed, as soon as I can gather enough cash to rebuild the Bellcote, the bells and the weathervane will be replaced and, of course, I shall then be committed to another effort to restore the entire roof where the slates are falling off like rain. But it's got a sort of guard along there, so you'll be able to walk along quite safely, without being decapitated. In any case, we're thoroughly insured in case anything like this should occur.

Now many of you probably have already seen where the Lewis memorial stone is, and the Professor and his brother are buried, but if not, you'll be able to look at it afterwards. As I'm addressing a conference avowedly Christian, I think we will, appropriately say a prayer in commemoration of Clive Staples Lewis, after all, he was a very remarkable, literary man and noted Christian apologist, before I actually say something about him as a parishioner. Would you like to kneel down and we'll say a prayer.

In the name of the Father and of the Son and of the Holy Ghost. Amen. Lord have mercy upon us; Christ have mercy upon us: Lord have mercy upon us. Our father, which art in heaven, hallowed be thy name; thy kingdom come, thy will be done, on earth as it is in heaven; give us this day our daily bread; and forgive us our trespasses as we forgive them that trespass against us; and lead us not into temptation, but deliver us from evil, for thine is the kingdom, the power and the glory, forever and ever. Amen.

The Lord be with you – and with thy spirit. Let us pray. O'God, the light of the souls of the faithful, assist our supplications: and grant unto thy servant, Clive Staples Lewis, and all whose bodies rest here in Christ, a place of refreshing, the blessedness of thy rest and the glory of everlasting life. Through Jesus Christ our Lord, who with thee and the Holy Ghost liveth and reigneth, ever one God, world without end. Amen. The Lord be with you – and with thy spirit let us bless the Lord. Thanks be to God; may the souls of the faithful, through the mercy of God, have rest in peace. Amen.

Will you sit down? What I'm going to say is something that I compiled long, long ago – not so long after the Professor had died. It's always a wise thing to do, especially when you discover someone is going to have lots of books written about them, otherwise you become tangled up entirely and think that the recollections of other people are, in fact, your recollections, even when they're not, so there are peculiar dangers about all of this. However, this is what I thought at the time. I still think the same now, of course, but it's one of those things.

Now it will be recalled that Clive Staples Lewis – with Mrs Moore, his adopted mother, and her daughter Maureen – came to live in Headington Quarry at the Kilns in 1930. Although the house itself was not very large – rather like a bungalow with an upper storey added (what people now term chalet) – it then stood, as it does now, well back from Kiln Lane but then in a piece of private ground some eight acres in extent.

The house acquired its name from two old brick kilns, then standing on the land not far from the house – for brick-making was a local industry in Headington Quarry during the nineteenth century, particularly after the quarries themselves had been worked out. This church, for example, was just dug out of the ground, outside there, the great cavity we now see, they just dug the church stone up put it up here and away they went. Built the whole lot for three thousand pounds, but brick-making was what they turned to. The little estate of the Lewis' comprised a tennis court, a wood and a pond – dignified by the name 'lake' or 'pool' – where some think the poet Shelley actually meditated. This secluded haven remained the Professor's residence until his death. The house itself can still be seen largely as it was, except for various internal alterations, and the erection of a brick garage in place of the former wooden structure.

C. S. Lewis' brother, Major Warren Hamilton Lewis (always called Warnie), arrived at the Kilns on retiring from the Army in 1932, and became part of that remarkable household presided over by Mrs Janie King-Moore. After the Major's death, the property was sold by Mrs Moore's daughter Maureen (by then Lady Dunbar) and other houses were then built on part of it – and that complex is what you see now as Lewis Close. I, in fact, never knew Mrs Janie King-Moore, as she died in 1951, the year before I arrived here and was buried in the churchyard in a grave, of all things, occupied by another Mrs Moore – namely Mrs Alice Hamilton Moore – described on her tombstone as 'Widow of Dr Robert Moore of Bush Mills, Ireland'. You may wonder how she came to be buried there; I indeed wonder the same myself. Consultation of the Burial Register, however, revealed the interesting fact that the Irish Mrs Moore, buried earlier in 1939, was also recorded as resident at the Kilns. One can only conclude that she may have been an inherited resident in the Kilns itself or lived in the bungalow, sometimes described as the summer house, which then stood in the grounds. My predecessor may have thought she was a relative, or he may not – I have no idea.

Headington Quarry village itself, it may be noted, didn't finally become part of the city of Oxford until 1929 – and that part of my parish where is situated the Kilns still remains in the County of Oxford and is not in the city of Oxford. Even the construction of the eastern by-pass road, about 1960, failed to destroy the country character of that little estate. The village character of Headington Quarry itself, which persists, was, of course, much stronger in the 1930s, particularly in its ecclesiastical aspect.

Professor Lewis and Major Lewis were, of course, known in Quarry generally as the Professor and the Major, and found themselves, therefore, at home in a community which took these two eccentric men just as they were found. My parishioners knew little about them and had no idea who they were. They looked like country men, walked around in old clothes, smoked pipes, visited public houses and fitted in happily with the local scene. Now, you will realise I am speaking of 'them' not 'him' – because I knew them together. My conversations were usually with two men who, when seen apart, seemed to share a likeness although one did not notice this so much when they were together. Their conversations sparkled and seemed to deal with any subject with equal brilliance. They were Irish born, being Ulstermen, and it is a fact clearly noted on their tombstone that they were born in Belfast.

Now, all of this was enjoyed by me in a different manner to other people as I knew them as parishioners who, however much they treated the vicar as an equal, never forgot who he actually was. The Professor was said to be a terror to his pupils, some of them have assured me of this, but that was a side of his character I never met at all. The Major was at one stage my Churchwarden. Previously, for many years, he'd been the correspondent of the Headington Quarry Church school managers of which the vicar, of course, was the chairman. In those early days the Major acted as the Professor's secretary, dealing with the vast correspondence from America and elsewhere. He always seemed to be sitting in the little room at the end of the passage down there at the Kilns, which you may see when we go up there, sitting there banging away at the typewriter.

Before the Professor's departure to Cambridge in 1954, they probably walked through my garden at some time during most days during term. I therefore often met them. My garden, of course, is not a public place, or it is not supposed to be, but I'll take you for a walk in it afterwards. It's important that you should see it, in a way, because it's the only way you can get any idea of how the Kilns stood in a vast open area and not as you will see it shortly. When I came to Headington Quarry, the Professor, originally agnostic, had already long before returned to the Church's fold. The Major, I believe, had probably taken that step at an earlier stage. When the Lewis establishment first appeared at the Kilns, Father Wilfred Thomas was then Vicar – you'll find his name on that list over there; a Catholic-minded priest in a village which had been influenced by the Oxford movement in various ways at least since 1867. Nevertheless, it was, interestingly enough, a village that had strong Methodist connections ante-dating the parish church erected in 1849. A new vicar of Low-Church outlook was instituted to this benefice by the evangel-ical Bishop Strong of Oxford in 1936, and that incumbent remained until 1947 when the return of the pendulum began with my prede-cessor in 1947, and reached the status quo ante on my appearance here later on.

People have often asked me what the Lewis' might have heard from the parish pulpit all those years, and I must confess that the theology must have been different at different stages but the brothers Lewis were not likely to have heard much of it. The Professor did not like organ music so their appearance at sung services were not so frequent and the modern mode of sermons at said masses too, has not even yet reached Holy Trinity here, where we continue precisely as before. The brothers appeared at 8am Holy Communion on Sundays without fail, unless they were away out of Oxford or something of that kind.

It was during the period of the 1939 War that the Professor, already known widely for his *Screwtape Letters,* became famous as a Christian apologist on account of his broadcast talks and lectures to the forces, leading up to the publication of *Mere Christianity* and other works of that kind. As far as I can tell this fact remained unknown to the majority of the faithful in Quarry, or they entirely failed to realise that this brilliant expositor was the man sitting concealed by that pillar in the aisle (the one with the flags on it); there's a little carved thing on the seat itself which shows where the Major sat, on the outside by the radiator and the Professor on the inside by the pillar, strategically placed so that they could see every-thing and be seen by no-one.

My parishioners in general, at that time, had not read either the science fiction about the sun and planets and so forth, or the chil-dren's stories. There were, of course, some people like Miss Griggs and Mrs Barnes-Griggs at Tewsfield – two elderly ladies who had read everything – but they were quite exceptional. I first met the Professor by the pond up there at the Kilns (which was a pond, probably sort of clay pit I think then), after I had been visiting Mrs Barnes-Griggs and Miss Griggs, the two elderly sisters-in-law I mentioned living at

Tewsfield. Tewsfield was a house, still there, but quite different now, which then shared a common drive with the Kilns. The only entrance they had, they had to pass the Kilns to get to it. That drive went up past the Kilns, up to their house and therefore, since they passed backwards and forwards, they knew the Lewises extremely well indeed.

I had, of course, already met the Major in church and I believe the first thing I ever said to the Professor was (I suppose it must sound very odd now), 'You must be the Churchwarden's brother'. We then promptly retired into the Kilns to the study at the end of the passage, to drink strong tea in large cups, sitting there among the books beside the ancient gramophone with its vast trumpet, engaged in cheerful talk about all kinds of things. My predecessor had warned me that the brothers would not talk about their books. The Major also, of course, had a literary flair of an historical kind and concentrated on seventeenth - and eighteenth-century France, a subject on which he possessed very considerable knowledge. At that time, the house was rather dark and dowdy, the walls were lined with books, old, large comfortable chairs were scattered around. The 1939 blackout curtains, impregnated with the smell of tobacco, still hung about the windows. The menage consisted of the general handyman/gardener/spare cook and everything else, namely Frank Paxford (Fred Paxford), together with a Mrs Miller, who performed as a cook on a daily basis, a dog (that is to say a large shaggy poodle, whose hair should have been cut but never was) and several cats who were also in evidence. A man's world indeed, in which it was easy to settle down once one got used to the Professor being called 'Jack' and the Major being called 'Warnie'.

C. S. Lewis, you will recall, was appointed Professor of Medieval and Renaissance Literature at Cambridge in 1954. From then on, during the term time, he spent weekdays in Cambridge and week-ends in Oxford, went backwards and forwards in taxis; he couldn't drive himself – he tried hard, but I told him once that he could never get out of bottom gear. Holidays in the vacation – they usually included for them trips to Ireland, the Major also going from time to time to Drogheda and to Cork.

When at home the Professor came to Holy Communion on Sundays and major saint's days in the week, daily, of course, in Holy week. The brothers adjusted the Sunday evening meal, their mealtimes were like the Laws of the Medes and Persians, but they were adjusted in time to come to evensong and address in Lent probably regarding the organ music, if not the address, as a suitable mortification for their sins. They always sat in the same place over there – a separate pew by the pillar, strategically placed, as I've already remarked, so that they could see the Alter and the Pulpit and not be seen! They left the church immediately after the blessing before anyone else could move. The only difficulty was that they were strangely clumsy with their hands, and sometimes dropped walking sticks, and could not quite manage the bogus medieval door latch. I solved that one by ensuring that the Verger (we had that kind of luxury in those far-off days)opened it for them. It's interesting to reflect that, in some respects, they seemed almost shy. In any case, they were not prepared to engage in conversation at that point. They vanished back to the Kilns and firmly shut the door.

For all kinds of reasons, Headington Quarry Parish Church is a religious entity and not a social one. There were not many social events, but those few which took place could usually rely on the presence of the Major and the Professor, both happily talking to those around. Both were well known in the Masons Arms public house – down there by the church gate!

C. S. Lewis – known, as I have said, to his intimates as Jack – usually arrived early to church services, and would sit quietly reading Psalms or other parts of the Prayer Book. I have often thought that *Meditations on the Psalms* occurred in my church. The 1662 Prayer Book is still used at Quarry. In any case, the regurgitations of the liturgical commission are not available during a lifetime.

The marriage of the Professor to Mrs Helen Joy Gresham, an American Jewess and the authoress of *Smoke in the Mountain*, took place very privately in the Oxford Registry Office in 1956, and was blessed by Father Peter Bide in the Wingfield Hospital in 1956, when she was thought to be dying. I myself ministered to her in the Churchill Hospital, where I was then Chaplain, although she had principally been a patient in the Wingfield Hospital over the road in the next parish. Mrs Lewis made a remarkable recovery, and I then found myself communicating her with him at the Kilns. At first she had a bed in the drawing room, but often she and the Professor could be found playing scrabble in Latin or in Anglo-Saxon. You had to be careful in which one you were invited to participate; their conversations sparkled in a notable way. She was, may I say, the first American lady of learning I'd ever met. A rather intimidating experience until one got used to the voice, the bulging eyes and the diabolical spectacles she often used to wear. Her health so improved at that time that she could get about and occupied another room on the ground floor. I believe one of their first excursions out was a visit in my car to the Vicarage for tea, when she demonstrated her pianistic accomplishments by playing with me two duets on two pianos!

Her arrival at the Kilns presaged a revolution. The house was done up, the furniture was re-upholstered and refurbished, even the blackout curtains disappeared and many improvements occurred. Her boys David and Douglas, were home at holiday times; indeed, they all came to church together. As is well known, this particular remission in her malady was of limited duration and, after a visit to Greece, her condition deteriorated rapidly and she died on 13th July 1960. She was cremated privately, the service at which I was present being taken by Dr Farrer, the then Warden of Keble. She is commemorated by a plaque, set up in one of the Cloisters at the Oxford Crematorium.

Life at the Kilns could not, in any respect, return to what it was before. The two Lewis brothers now had a pair of teenage boys, David and Douglas Gresham, as a constituent part of their household. Professor Lewis was indeed bereft, as, in certain respects, is indicated to readers of *A Grief Observed* and, as always in circumstances of this kind, one wondered how his health would stand up to such a strain. In 1961 he was not so well, I communicated him at home on several occasions. In the following year, '62, in some respects he seemed better. He was still travelling to and from Cambridge, but on the whole did not seem to be anything like so active. Major Lewis seemed in a little better state I suppose and went off to Ireland for long periods. The domestic administration of the Kilns went on much as before. That was about the time of the *Honest to God* controversy. Conversations with the Professor naturally touched on such matters, as also on prayer, matters theological arising out of sermons and so forth. The Professor was what one would call properly and strictly orthodox, like the old Church of Ireland – much sounder and more united in theology. Too frequently this tends to do the precise opposite. *Letters to Malcolm* (No. 12) reports an actual conversation and prayer with me. I always felt that conversations with the Professor were purposeful, never mere chatter or pleasant nothingness. He was a very logical thinker, not allowing anyone to get away with slipshod arguments. It was about this time in 1963 that Father Walter Hooper, then a layman, appeared from America. I believe they had been in touch by correspondence over quite a period. He was very knowledgeable about the Professor's writings. The Professor, he thought he knew more about them than he did himself. They clearly took to one another at once. They appeared at Church together, they were always seen together and they really got on pretty wonderfully. The Major, again, was away in Ireland and not well. In July '63 the Professor was indeed seriously ill in the Acland Home and the Radcliffe Infirmary. Walter Hooper took me down to Keble to confer with Dr Farrer about this strange situation we found ourselves in. It was not possible to get the Major back; there were no relatives in place. The Major, in fact, was also in hospital at the other end. Happily, the Professor, after being annointed by Father Watts, who was then the Precentor at the Cathedral recovered and in time returned to the Kilns, with a male nurse temporarily in attendance and Walter Hooper permanently added to the household. Lewis' heart attack and its complications led to his resignation from the Cambridge professorship. I then began communicating him at home on a fortnightly basis, which continued, in fact, until his death. The Major had recovered and was back in circulation again. In the nature of this case, this was a period when I had longer conversations with the Professor than probably at any stage – covering, of course, the usual field of spiritual matters, questions concerning the faith, the problems besetting the Church of England, dangers of change, revision of services and so forth. Lewis had a solid preference that the prayers of the Church should be familiar so that one should be free to meditate on them, to sink into them to, take them as one's own. Hence, his interest in the quotations from ancient fathers – St Augustine and the Psalms; all those kind of things which I often mentioned in the Sermons. He was a man of deep devotion. For example, when receiving Holy Communion and, of course, in long-standing affection, never failing to put Mrs Moore's name on the list of the faithful departed for Commemoration on All Souls' day. He was a very humble man, self-effacing and never speaking of his remarkable talents or of his services to other people. One could note his care in answering letters, his generosity in giving money away, not I believe, so much to institutions but rather to individuals he could help – scholars, clergy, all sorts of people.

His death was, on the whole, even then unexpected. I'd only communicated him a few days previously when he seemed much the same, that is, there was nothing notably amiss, yet he died suddenly on Friday, 22nd November 1963 at about half past five in the afternoon. Later that evening, the Major was running about looking for me, forgetful that it was the Anniversary day of the Parish Church's Consecration in 1849. I was actually presiding over a Parish party unaware of both of the death of the Professor and the assassination of President Kennedy at Dallas, on the same day. The Professor's funeral took place in the parish church here and he was buried in the churchyard. No announcement of any kind had been made about him. The Major wouldn't announce anything, he was prostrate and indeed wasn't even at the service. He had previously said there should be no flowers, but the foot of the coffin and subsequently the grave, was graced by a sheaf of flowers brought to the funeral service by Dr Nicholas Zhernof. The impression of Peter Hailey that there was a candle burning on the coffin was mistaken, although there were, of course, the customary candles standing round the coffin just there, and I suppose during the procession to the grave, from a distance, the candles of the acolytes accompanying the processional cross might, have caused such an illusion.

The Professor's body had been received into the church the night before, and I said Requiem on the day of the burial, Tuesday, 26th. His memorial service took place in Magdalen College Chapel on the following Saturday, 30th. His tombstone bearing the quotation from *King Lear*, 'men must endure their going hence', was not laid exactly out as one would have desired, as the Major seemed unable to realise that when he himself was buried something more would have to be added underneath. Happily the Major lived for another ten years, which gave him plenty of time to think up something which could appear. Clergymen are always faced with this problem that they have to try to make inscriptions on tombstones read sensibly from beginning to end. His grave, of course, became a place of pilgrimage for many people, particularly from the new world. There's no particular memorial to him in the Parish, although perhaps some day I suppose something might appear.

I think that is all you can hear on this tape. I think you'd probably like to travel round the church and, if it's not pouring with rain, then go and look at the grave. Then perhaps you'd like to take a walk round my garden before you get back into the coach, wherever it may be. That's solved your problems, or do you want to do anything else?

The Grave of Mrs Janie King-Moore

The grave of Mrs Janie King-Moore and Alice Hamilton, the lady with whom she is buried, can also be found in the churchyard of Holy Trinity about thirty yards away from the Lewis brothers' grave and towards the right-hand perimeter wall, assuming, that is, that you are standing with your left shoulder at the head of the Lewis tombstone. The inscription on the poorly maintained grave shared by the two Mrs Moores, which I believe should equally be looked after by the C. S. Lewis Foundation because of the related importance, reads:

In memory of

Alice Hamilton

Widow of Dr Robert Moore
of Bush Mills, Ireland

Born Nov 20th 1853
Died Nov 2nd 1939

sleep after toil, port after stormy seas
also of

Janie King Moore

Died Jan 12th 1951

Warren 'Warnie' Hamilton Lewis (1895–1973)

Warnie was Churchwarden at Holy Trinity during the years 1953–7 and like Jack, had his regular seat in church near the pillar to St George in the north aisle, only he would always sit on the outside of the pew nearest the radiator as you see it today (although in those days the radiator would not have been there). Warnie was three years older than Jack and a prolific writer also, but he concentrated on seventeenth - and eighteenth-century France, of which he was considered to be very knowledgeable. He published several books of his own, including *The Splendid Century Life in the France of Louis XIV* and *Levantine Adventurer: The travels and missions of the Chevalier d'Arvieux, 1653–1697*. Despite being Jack's secretary, dealing with the correspondence from America and elsewhere and using a typewriter which, compared with today's technology, would have you wondering how on earth he managed. The actual typewriter that he used is on show at the Kilns. (if you are ever lucky enough to do a tour of the house to see it!) To describe the typewriter as an ancient piece of equipment is an understatement; it is, however, the only remaining original item on show in the house. Not even Lewis' furniture survived, so surely, one is entitled to ask what happened to it all, perhaps the C. S. Lewis Foundation know?

It was 1932 before Major Warren Hamilton Lewis, Royal Army Service Corps, retired from the Army and then returned to live at the Kilns with Jack and Mrs Moore (died 1951), until his death on 9th April 1973.

Note: During a recent visit to the Kilns, Kim Gilnett said that, we (presumably meaning the Foundation), would like to work more closely with you, and told me that an original sofa from the former Lewis home is in the attic awaiting restoration. I accept the offer 'to work more closely' as a small step forward in our quest to keep the Lewis legacy alive.

Oxford Crematorium Ltd.

After the inevitable photographs of the beautiful Holy Trinity church and churchyard you will leave by the gates at the end of the path where you arrived. Turn right at the top of the slight incline about seventy-five yards away and follow the narrow Trinity Road for about 200 yards until you reach the Six Bells public house (another Lewis watering hole), on your left. Follow the bend in the road to the left until you reach the 'T' junction 75 yards away at which you turn right to join the dual carriageway. At the dual carriageway turn left (with Risinghurst Estate now in front of you), and proceed to the roundabout where you need to take the fourth exit signposted towards Oxford Crematorium, Stanton-St-John and Beckley which will be on your left. Follow the road downhill which will be Bayswater Road.

Note: As I write, plans to install a new traffic system at the Headington roundabout are being considered but regardless of what the Planning Department's final decision is for the roundabout follow the road signs to Oxford Crematorium as described above.

It is at Oxford Crematorium that the ashes of Helen Joy Lewis were scattered; it being Joy's wish that her body be cremated. (Joy was cremated in her married name despite the memorial plaque referring to Helen Joy Davidman). Stay on this road travelling down Bayswater Road for about six hundred yards until you get to Oxford Crematorium entrance, which is situated on the left as a slight incline in the road becomes apparent. I would like to remind visitors at this stage that Oxford Crematorium Ltd is privately owned and, although the Crematorium Superintendent has no objection to visitors to the Garden of Remembrance, there is, in fact, a service held at the Crematorium every fifteen minutes during weekdays and sometimes on a Saturday. Photographs are permitted in the Garden of Remembrance; however, your consideration for those who have lost loved ones would be appreciated.

If you are driving to Oxford Crematorium, ample provision is made available for free parking of your vehicle on the right-hand side as you enter. However, on entering you will need to travel towards the Crematorium chapels first, before turning right and then parking on the right, please do not park in the reserved bays! Sadly, even in the Crematorium grounds, an amount of vandalism exists whilst vehicles are left unattended with car windows being smashed and bags, cameras and other valuables being stolen so do secure your vehicle, hiding away any valuables etc. Walk towards the buildings which will now be slightly to your front left-hand side. Stay on this road but still keep to the right, which will take you behind the waiting room/rest room area (the rest room is closed at 4pm daily should you need to use this facility). By now it is possible to see Cloister 2 in the Garden of Remembrance to the right of the Crematorium chapels. You will find the plaque dedicated to the memory of Helen Joy Davidman situated in the bottom far right-hand corner on the right-hand pillar, under two tall verigated leylandi trees which stand out against the red of the copper beech and pine trees that determine the Crematorium boundary.

The Helen Joy Davidman Memorial Plaque

A poem called 'Epitaph', which was written by Lewis, can be seen cut into a marble plaque at Oxford Crematorium. The size of the plaque is approximately eighteen inches by twelve inches, the inscription reads as follows:

Remember
Helen Joy Davidman
D. July 1960
loved wife of
C. S. Lewis
here the whole world (stars, water, air
reflected in a single mind)
like cast off clothes was left behind
in ashes, yet with hope that she,
re-born from holy poverty,
in lenten lands, hereafter may
resume them on her easter day.

(Poems by C. S. Lewis copyright© C. S. Lewis Pte. Ltd. Reprinted by permission.)

For knowledge and/or a photograph of the location (known as B4), where Mrs Joy Lewis' ashes were scattered at Oxford Crematorium you need to be south of Cloister 2. To find the area, the following directions will help. As you face Joy's memorial plaque you need to turn left out of Cloister 2 and left again through the archway. Walk about 20 yards bearing right on the lawn and look for a large oak tree which is to your front left about two hundred yards away. (Imagine the time ten to six on a clock face for an idea of the angle.) To the left of the large oak tree you will see four magnolia trees in the shape of a square and to the left of the magnolia trees is the rose bed known as B4. The ashes of Mrs Joy Lewis as recorded by Oxford Crematorium Ltd were scattered between the magnolia trees and B4. If you are still unsure refer to the photograph section in this guide.

Helen Joy Davidman was an American Jewess and her religion would strictly forbid the act of cremation. However, it was Joy's own wish just hours before her death that her body be cremated. One assumes therefore that she was very happy converting to Christianity. However, I would have thought that it could have been arranged for her ashes to have at least been scattered or interred nearer to Jack at Holy Trinity Church in Headington Quarry, albeit Jack would live on for another two and a half years! As it is, there is no reference to Helen Joy Lewis at Lewis' tombstone, nor yet a reference to C. S. Lewis' tombstone at Oxford Crematorium!

As you leave Oxford Crematorium by way of the exit gate as opposed to the entry where you came in, you need to turn right. Follow the road back down Bayswater Road and up the other side to Headington roundabout again. Take the second exit signposted to Cowley. Please remember that at the time of writing there is talk of a new traffic light system being introduced at this roundabout. In any case, follow the road signs directing you to Cowley on the Ring Road. Once on the Ring Road and just before the first set of traffic lights about three hundred yards away, turn left on the short slip road to Risinghurst Estate, turn left again immediately and then right at the 'T' junction of Green Road and Kiln Lane, about fifty yards away. Continue along Kiln Lane taking note of Shelley Close on the right-hand side. It is believed that poet Shelley enjoyed the peace and quiet of Lewis' lakeside, hence, perhaps, Shelley Close! The fourth turn on the right in Kiln Lane is Lewis Close. At this stage it is probably best to park your vehicle in Kiln Lane, or the surrounding area and then walk into Lewis Close, at the top of which and almost hidden away behind the silver birch trees on the right-hand side is the red-slate tiled roof that will confirm you have arrived at the former home of C. S. Lewis. (Unless you have arranged an internal viewing thirty minutes will be sufficient time here.) It was ten years after the death of Jack in 1963 that Warnie died and by the mid-1970s the whole estate was valued at just over seventy-five thousand pounds, with various bequests going to those who had served the brothers over the years.

The Victorian Stamps, Wheaton College, Illinois and The Will

Under the terms of Warnie's Last Will and Testament, all of Jack's letters, photographs and manuscripts were left to Wheaton College in Illinois, USA. Why? Because they were the first to ask for them. With this in mind, I wrote to Wheaton College and the Foundation, enquiring whether they had any letters from the former Lewis home that were in envelopes where the stamps had been removed. They wrote back saying something like, 'We are unaware of the existence of such envelopes and, in any case, they would be of no significance.' However, I shall explain. One day, whilst sitting on the floor of Dougie's bedroom swapping coins, cigarette cards and stamps or just being boys amongst the schoolboy shambles of his room, Dougie handed to me a bundle of envelopes measuring about six inches by four inches. They were tied together neatly and secured with a piece of pink wool. I pulled at the bow and each of the envelopes had a Victorian penny red stamp on them. I remember Dougie saying, 'You can't have the letters inside, they belong to my father but you can have the stamps'. At the time I never thought to ask Dougie whether he meant his biological father (in fact, the word 'biological' probably wasn't even in my vocabulary) or Jack. However, I carefully removed all of the stamps and duly mounted them in my stamp album, where they remained untouched for nearly fifty years!

It was only when I began doing the C. S. Lewis Tours that I went to the stamp album again and looked more closely at the postmarks

– Killarney 1868. Yes, thirty years before C. S. Lewis was born! So who could those letters have been from? Although I still do not have the answer, I suppose a DNA test would at least prove that they were from the Lewis family because somebody must have licked the back of the stamp. Maybe they were from Jack's parents or even grandparents! So, although, I still have the stamps, where are those letters and envelopes today and more interestingly perhaps, what would the contents have revealed about life before C. S. Lewis? The idea of a DNA test on the stamps became a distinct possibility because, just recently, as I was introduced to the name of Joan Lewis-Murphy, a second cousin to C. S. Lewis, who also happens to live in Oxfordshire.

On another occasion whilst in Dougie's bedroom I watched him as he sat peeling the chequered cardboard outer from a 9mm garden gun cartridge (the gun he used for shooting rats in the barn), to enable him to use the lead pellets as weights for his fishing line. He threw the copper-coloured cap on the bedroom floor thinking it was now spent. I said, 'Dougie, do you know that cap is still live?' He replied, 'No, it's not', which was the signal for me to prove him wrong. I picked it up and we ran across to the barn where I laid the cap on an old steel roller that Fred used for flattening down worm mounds on the lawns. I picked up half of a house brick and swiftly brought it down on the cap and, of course, it went bang! 'Told you so,' I yelled with excitement, but my glee was short-lived because metal fragments had shot out from between the brick and the garden roller which had then entered my inside right knee area. I ran home not knowing what to expect but was rushed to the Radcliffe Infirmary in Oxford were an X-ray revealed three pieces of shrapnel. The hospital decided not to operate, believing they would work their own way out in due course. I don't know to this day if I am still the proud owner of those metal fragments, although a doctor who did the tour recently said, 'Get another X-ray done Ron, I'll bet they are still in the same place.'

Access to the Former Lewis Home

By now you will be realising that it is possible to gain entry to the former home of this literary giant, although currently very difficult, so for those who wish to attempt the almost impossible I make no apology for trying to steer you in the right direction. A good start would be to contact the Head Resident at the Kilns. The direct dial telephone number is listed on page 11; alternatively you can go to the internet webpage http://www.cslewis.org which will give you direct contact with the Foundation in Redlands, California. But don't be holding your breath whilst waiting for a response because I have found them less than helpful and they rarely return emails. They appear to do nothing to encourage visitors; maybe the following letters are an indication of why. The following rare email arrived from Stan Mattson, Founder and President of the C. S. Lewis Foundation, on 4th September 2003, it reads:

Dear Ron,

I trust you have been enjoying a good summer of activity in Oxford notwithstanding temperatures on the high side, to put it mildly. I'm writing to request your assistance in our efforts to properly manage the large number of visitors hoping to visit the kilns.

As you know, the home is located in a residential neighborhood and does, itself, serve as home year round to residents engaged in the study of Lewis and related authors. Although it is understandably and appropriately of great interest to many it is neither a museum nor public property. In our sincere desire to accommodate the desires of our many visitors without compromising the normal private lives of the home's residents, it is essential that any and all visits to the kilns be arranged well in advance of the desired date. This can be accomplished easily by contacting our Head residents at the kilns, currently Mr & Mrs Brandon Galliher, at 01865-741865. If at all possible, they will pleased to confirm all appropriate arrangements. (Please note that the recommended contribution towards the support of the home is £5.00 per person.) Should it not be possible for you to arrange an agreed upon appointment with Brandon (which I would anticipate would be the exception), I would respectfully ask you to honour the privacy and announced policy of the household, restricting your viewing from the curb, taking care not to enter the grounds.

I trust you will appreciate the fact that our request is one shared of necessity with all tour guide leaders, and that it in no way reflects anything but our desire to manage the affairs of this special property in a way that accommodates as many as possible without making life unbearable for those who live there year round. Enjoying a cup of well-earned tea at the end of an exhausting day only to discover someone peering in the window at you or making their way through your garden unannounced can be more than a bit unsettling, as I'm sure you and can well imagine.

Should you have any questions about any aspect of this, do please feel completely free to raise them via return e-mail.

Cordially,

Stan

J. Stanley Mattson, Ph.d.
Founder and President
C. S. Lewis Foundation
P.O. 8008, Redlands, ca 92375
Tel: (909) 793-0949

I responded with the following email:

Dear Stan,

I refer to your email dated 4th September 2003.

Firstly, I would like to thank you for taking the trouble to contact me, because over the years it has proved very difficult to reach your organisation. Despite my emails (the last one was asking for a return link to my webpage), nobody seems to want to talk to me. For the record, I have had a link to your page now for a long time and as my page is no 1 in the search engine lists, I have no doubt that the C. S. Lewis Foundation•has benefited from it. So how about returning the compliment?

As for all visits to the Kilns being pre-arranged, it wouldn't work. I would dearly love to be able to show pilgrims inside the property that I know so well but it would mean that each time I had a tour booked, and that's almost daily and at different times, I would need to telephone Brandon or his wife. They would soon get very tired of me, so I do the next best thing. I take visitors to the former Lewis home explaining that it is a private residence, asking that they respect this. Generally, they comply with my request. However, on two recent visits, one when a 'seminar' was obviously taking place and the other when fellow Americans staying at the Kilns invited my visitors to the home, by talking to them from a distance that was soon reduced as a result. I suspect the 'complaint' that it appears you may have had has come as a direct result of these incidents.

I understand also that it is not a public place but feel that it should be. I believe the National Trust should have a hand in what goes on at the Kilns because of its importance to both our countries, although I also admit that many 'Brits' still don't know who C. S. Lewis was. In a recent survey that I carried out for a book that I have written, called *A Guide to the C. S. Lewis Tour in Oxfordshire*, 70% thought that C. S. Lewis wrote Alice in Wonderland!

In the book I call for a fitting memorial to be erected to the memory of Jack and Joy as man and wife, perhaps in Magdalen College grounds and paid for by the Lewis Awareness Fund, which could be set up. Further, to then purchase all properties that have been built on what was the orchard, demolish them and dig up the road also. We should then restore the Kilns to its former glory. I have documented 'how it was' during the late 1950s, when Dougie and I played there as boys. The C. S. Lewis Foundation would still own the Kilns, as it presumably does, with the National Trust providing support where required.

My vehicular tour takes up to three hours and brings great delight to those who travel; indeed, 'Tour Reviews' on my webpage say it all. Perhaps you can find time to take a peep. I have a set of keys to Holy Trinity Church, another place of immense feelings for those dedicated people, some of whom travel from the USA literally only to do the tour.

I still have 52 Victorian stamps that came from envelopes in the Lewis household postmarked Killarney 1868. Dougie said, 'They [meaning the letters inside] belong to my father but you can't have them.' I settled for the stamps and decanters that Dougie and I found in the attic that were then given to me by Jack. I remember well Dougie asking, 'Jack, can Ron take these home?' Jack twisted in his chair under the window, looked over his shoulder•and with a flick of his hand, on an extended•arm said 'Yes'. I•still have these items also. He was a 'gentle man' as well as a gentleman!•

I would wish to work more closely with your organisation and if you like, become the 'official' C. S. Lewis Tour. In those circumstances I could see more visitors coming, which would then fill every tour, which in turn would allow for the all important pre-arranged visits to be properly announced, simply because a set time daily would become the norm.•

I hope I have not bored you with my thoughts, Stan, and look forward to a closer working relationship.

As a final point, I am considering making a video and/or DVD of my tour. In return for your co-operation the Foundation could benefit.•What are your thoughts?•

Regards

Ron

To this day I am still waiting for a response. (During our meeting, which took place on 28th August 2004, Stan Mattson apologised for not answering that email. He said 'I get lots of emails and cannot answer them all. There is only myself and one other lady available.' My thoughts that the C. S. Lewis Foundation of Redlands, California, was a huge organisation had collapsed in an instant.

Observations, Questions and Answers?

1. Try getting an appointment to enter the former home of C. S. Lewis. I have managed to gain entry three or four times in four years! Why is that?

2. Why did the recommended contribution towards the support of the home rise from £3.00 the previous year to £5.00 this? Surely, it should be left to the individual to make a donation as they feel appropriate, or as they can afford?

3. How are the donations used and/or recorded? After our meeting on 28th August 2004 I now have a better understanding of how some of the funds are distributed, but don't agree with it. I wonder if it could affect the 501 (c) 3 status that the Foundation currently enjoys?

4. Why doesn't the C. S. Lewis Foundation link back to my webpage on the internet? My belief is that they don't want me to show visitors where the former home is. (Our meeting of 28th August 2004 also provided the answer.) Stan Mattson said that people involved with the Foundation were of a higher academic level and would not be interested in my tour. He added 'I would never link to your webpage.' I suggested he looked at the 'Tour Reviews' at www.cslewistours.com and I have since removed the C. S. Lewis Foundation link from my webpage! I have also added a note explaining that my only involvement with the Foundation is for regular communication

in an attempt to get the former Lewis home recognised with a plaque, that it be open for all visitors, and ultimately that the National Trust gets involved to save Lewis' former home for the benefit of our future generations.

5. The second paragraph of the letter from Stan Mattson, I believe says it all: 'I'm writing to request your assistance in our efforts to properly manage the large number of visitors hoping to visit the Kilns,' – 'hoping to visit the Kilns' being the operative words. I can only hope that our relationship gets better. Somehow with my vision of total restoration for the Kilns already hitting the buffers, I don't think so. Sad then, that so many Americans who have done the tour with me offer their help in restoring the Kilns to its former glory making comments like, 'We would be honoured to organise working parties to come over and help you, Ron.'

With regard to my vision of total restoration, I have no doubt whatsoever that the C. S. Lewis Foundation will be quick to defend their position saying, 'but we have already restored and renovated the Kilns.' Wrong in my opinion. I believe they have only chipped away at the tip of the iceberg despite nine years of restoration and in fact, have probably taken a few steps backwards, if you consider that they have installed central heating, for example. This clearly is for modern day comfort of the international students and others who live there year in, year out! They have started the journey with the former home and that is all because today it looks precisely like what they have created, a modern and comfortable home that is anything but the way it was when the Lewis brothers lived there.

The eight acres of land purchased solely by Mrs Janie King-Moore during 1930 is today broken up into three plots and each plot needs major work to restore it as near as is possible to its original condition.

Who Did Purchase the Kilns?

To avoid any misunderstanding, Mrs Janie King-Moore purchased the Kilns in 1930 with her sole name on the deeds. However, it is often reported that she bought the Kilns with Jack and Warnie, which, depending on how you wish to interpret it, could mean that they were in her company when she agreed to buy it or that they each made a financial contribution towards it. Maybe Jack and Warnie did help financially and my understanding is that they did actually contribute jointly one thousand, two hundred pounds in cash – either way, the fact is that Mrs Moore allowed Jack and Warnie a 'Right of Life Tenancy', which meant that they were able to stay there for as long as they wished, even after her death.

Frank (Fred) Paxford (1898–1979)

Frank Paxford (Fred) was the spare cook and the general maintenance man. He was also, I believe, Dougie's mentor and a good friend to us boys generally. We probably pushed his patience to the limit many times but he never really complained and he was always there to show us how to get best results out of whatever we were doing at the time. Fred often wore a blue and white pin-striped shirt which was grubby most times, but to change the collar was to change the shirt because in those days the collars were attached or detached by studs and, although a clean collar might have looked better, it didn't do much to take away the smell of the body odour!

It was in the kitchen one day, whilst Fred was presumably preparing tea for Jack and/or Warnie, that I saw Fred take hold of a loaf of bread in his left hand. He was holding it close to his chest as he took a large knife and brought it round onto the front of the loaf. After removing the crust he put so much butter on what was to be the next slice of bread that I have likened it many times since to a builder laying a cement fillet around the top of a chimney stack. He repeated the cutting action and ended up with a slice of bread so thin that it had to be picked off the top of the loaf with the blade of the knife rather than by hand for fear of it breaking apart. So, thinking back, Jack and/or Warnie liked butter and bread in that order. Our dear old friend Fred Paxford died in 1979, in the village of Churchill, Oxfordshire.

Other members of the household who Fred cared about included the flea-ridden cat called Ginger, who had no teeth, and the grey/black standard poodle that never saw a bath unless you consider a dunking in the lake from time to time acceptable and who only very occasionally had his coat clipped! In fact, I would say that most of the dog and cat hairs ended up on the sofas and carpets throughout the house. What a good housekeeper Mrs Miller was, eh? Trusted housekeeper and cook Mrs Maud Miller was typical in dress and style of those days. Thinking back, she wasn't very tall, a little on the dumpy side and nearly always wore a dull flower-print cotton apron that seemed to wrap around her ample body at least twice! Her silver/grey hair somehow seemed to balance precariously on her head but was no doubt secured with hair nets and hairgrips. Without any doubt Mrs Miller was stricter with Dougie than his own mother, Jack, Warnie or Fred Paxford which I suppose didn't come as any surprise to Dougie for she wasn't at the top of his Christmas card list either!

The Last Will and Testament of Warren Hamilton Lewis

In Warnie's Will, the total value of the estate being worth just over seventy-five thousand pounds, Mrs Miller was left five thousand pounds (must have been some cook for that percentage, even if her cleaning skills left something to be desired), but she and her husband Leonard had to occupy the Kilns rent free for six months after his death, to which Lady Maureen Daisy Dunbar (Mrs Janie King-Moore's daughter) had to agree, to receive one thousand pounds. Presumably Leonard and Maud Miller were there to protect the property whilst matters were brought to a conclusion.

Also in Warnie's Will was a bequest of five hundred pounds to the Rev. Walter McGeHee Hooper, then of Wadham College, Oxford. To go back a little Walter Hooper (1931–) had been immersing himself in everything C. S. Lewis wrote since he first discovered his writings. Lewis and Hooper began corresponding in 1954, and after a while Lewis invited Hooper to visit him in Oxford. Hooper was teaching English in the University of Kentucky, and in June 1963 he arrived in Oxford for his first visit with Lewis. They met at the Kilns on 7th June and got on so well they were soon meeting three times a week, going to Church together on Sundays. Lewis was in desperate need of someone to help with his vast correspondence, and he asked Hooper if he would become his secretary – beginning immediately. Hooper moved into the Kilns and was able to give Lewis a good deal of help before he had to go back to Kentucky to teach one final term. It was agreed that he would return to Oxford in January 1964 to take up his position as secretary. As it turned out, Lewis died on 22 November 1963, when Hooper was still in Kentucky. However, he came back over, and in January 1964 Warnie invited him to edit his brother's literary remains – a job he continues to this day in his capacity of Literary Advisor to the Estate of C. S. Lewis.

In 1965 Walter Hooper was ordained in the Church of England, and between 1965 and 1971 he served as Chaplain to both Wadham and Jesus Colleges, Oxford. In 1988 he converted to the Roman Catholic Church, and he is now a Roman Catholic layman. During all this time he has never stopped working for the Lewis Estate, and some time ago he began editing *The Collected Letters of C. S. Lewis* in three volumes. The first two volumes have been published, and he is working on the final one.

The Lewis Awareness Fund

With regard to my vision of total restoration at the Kilns, this travel guide will hopefully help. As the book is published I will launch the fund with some of the profits from expected sales, thus I will open an account to start the ball rolling. I hope it will allow like-minded individuals to contact me via my webpage with a view to making a donation to the fund, which, over many years to come, would argue the case for reinstatement of all that existed from 1930 onwards at the Kilns.

Having read of my vision and my hope within this guide I have absolutely no doubt that many groups of volunteers from America will seize upon the opportunity to be part of the restoration and organise themselves into working parties, indeed, as some have already offered. Despite this, my personal opinion is that the National Trust needs to become involved to protect the site now, for the benefit of future generations because C. S. Lewis continues to change the hearts and minds of millions of people throughout the world. I also believe that the C. S. Lewis Foundation is very wrong in their attitude and opinion towards this property and that this is one of the most important historical sites in the land which should at least be restored to its former glory of the 1950s and then to be opened to visitors for all to see how this most gentle man lived in comparative squalor. I believe that pilgrims from afar would be interested not only in helping but would see it as an honour to repay the comfort that C. S. Lewis has brought to so many.

Surely, they would like to see for themselves how the rooms throughout the property were decorated. The nicotine-stained ceilings which have apparently already been recreated (but they are not like they were in the 1950s) and the stains on the walls, which today we could reproduce. Just how was this typically English country cottage decorated? How big was the library and was it really full of books held together with cobwebs – I can tell you, yes, it was dirty! What was on the floor – linoleum, quarry tiles, carpets or nothing at all? What was the furniture like? How did they cook? Where did Jack and Warnie sit whilst writing? Which room did Joy occupy during her illness? The list goes on and for those of you who already know, there is no longer a yearning. However, for those who want to know, it is surely an experience to look forward to and one for which most would be prepared to pay. With the fund available we could even look forward to the suggested appropriate memorial to Mr and Mrs C. S. Lewis.

In an ideal situation, we need to purchase the houses in Lewis Close from their private owners, built on what was once the orchard, the former Lewis home from the C. S. Lewis Foundation and the lake and woodland from the Wildlife Trust. In the event that any part of the former eight-acre plot and/or buildings are unavailable for purchase, for whatever reason, I would most certainly advocate compulsory purchase. At the launch of this guide I will be in contact with the National Trust in an attempt to pursue the aforementioned and would consider it an honour if my old school friend Dougie Gresham were to 'jump ship' and become involved also.

The Glass Decanters

With restoration under way perhaps also I could be encouraged to return what may be the only genuine surviving chattels from the former Lewis home. I am referring to the fifty-two Victorian stamps from the envelopes and the whiskey and wine decanters that Dougie and I found in the attic, one day, as boys. We were upstairs and noticed a trap door in the wall of a bedroom where we were playing which we removed to explore the darkness beyond. With a hand-held torch that was no bigger than my index finger today. We searched the attic but there was nothing else up there. I asked Dougie if he thought Jack would let me take the decanters home to my parents. 'Let's go and ask him,' said Dougie. We put the trap door back and went downstairs to the lounge where Jack was working at his desk in the left-hand corner of the room. Holding the two glass decanters out in front of him Dougie asked Jack, 'Can Ron take these home to his parents?' Jack merely twisted at the hips, looked over his shoulder and with his arm outstretched muttered his agreement, a nod of the head and a flick of the back of the hand as if to say, 'Don't bother me now boys, I'm writing a book called *Mere Christianity*.' Well alright, I added the *Mere Christianity* bit but who knows what he could have been writing and the fact remains that I still have those very precious decanters and the stamps. Thinking back, I told my parents that the decanters came from Major Lewis' house because, locally, he was the better known of the two brothers, who bore a strange likeness. Unless you actually saw them together and that wasn't a particularly regular occurrence despite what others might suggest, it was easy to mistake one for the other. As for Mrs Janie King-Moore being the owner of the Kilns – she wasn't even mentioned in my days. It seems the few short years from 1951 when she died were now distant and had already taken their toll.

Jack and Warnie would sit at a desk in the bay windows at the back of the property looking out onto a framework of rustic wood fencing covered with pink roses. A low red-brick wall which still supports the garden and the lawns completed a fantastic view to the woodland beyond.

The Sinking of the Lewis Punt

C. S. Lewis owned a punt, which was moored on the lake to the rear of his former home at the Kilns. However, during the early 1950s two youth's from the adjacent housing development decided it would be fun to sink it. They proceeded to load it with heavy timbers from the surrounding woodlands until it went down. The water, I am told, appeared almost 'boiling' as the air beneath now escaped to the surface. What was left of the punt was recovered from the murkey depths by volunteers who, working on behalf of the C. S. Lewis Foundation, tied ropes around their waists before venturing into the lake during 1994. The head of restoration at the Kilns told me during 1994 that the punt would be stored away in the attic for renovation one day!

Homeward Bound : The Ampleforth Arms Public House

In leaving the Kilns at the bottom of Lewis Close turn right and travel about two hundred yards before you turn left into Grovelands Road, turn immediately left again into Collinwood Road and at the first set of crossroads about two hundred yards away you will see the Ampleforth Arms public house (drive by only on tour). The Amp, as it is known locally, is on the right-hand side of the crossroads and is the pub that Lewis and Tolkien had a beer in and where Dougie and I fetched Lewis' beer in the cider bottles! My wife Anna and I gave up the pub life in 1994 and came out of the Ampleforth Arms after we realised that we were never going to bed the same day!

With the tour now completed, and assuming you need to return to Oxford City, continue on down Collinwood Road for about three hundred yards until you get to the A40 dual carriageway. Turn left and travel towards Headington roundabout remembering that plans are in hand to change the roundabout, to a proposed 'traffic light' system. Continue on the A40 over the roundabout or traffic lights when installed, for about one and a half miles until you get to the Marston turn just before the bridge, where you need to turn left on the slip road towards Marston and Elsfield. Within about three hundred yards you will need to turn left at the 'T' junction, the road signs will direct you to Elsfield. Continue for about two hundred yards and turn right into Marsh Lane. Continue along Marsh Lane until you reach the mini-roundabout about five hundred yards away and then turn right. You are now in Cherwell Drive and travelling towards Oxford city (north). You need to stay on this road for one and a half miles until you reach the next 'T' junction, which will be the Banbury Road traffic lights at which you need to turn left towards Oxford city. Follow the Banbury Road into Oxford city for another one and a half miles and you are now approaching St Giles thoroughfare. This is the section of wide road with the Eagle and Child public house now on your right-hand side behind the trees. Another five hundred yards or so and you need to turn right at the traffic lights to finish up at the Randolph Hotel where the tour began.

The Radcliffe Infirmary

The foundation stone for the hospital was laid on 27th August 1761 but five years later, after the death of the original architect, Stiff Leadbetter, the work was completed by John Sanderson. As you face the hospital's main entrance from Woodstock Road and with the fountain in the middle of the courtyard, look to the right to see the hospital chapel, which was built in 1864 and where one can reasonably assume that Joy's body would have been taken soon after her death in 1960.

The Radcliffe Infirmary (drive by only), is about a ten-minute walk away from the Randolph Hotel in Beaumont Street and about five hundred yards north of the Eagle and Child public house in St Giles. At the time of writing, my understanding is that Oxford Brookes University have negotiated a deal with the Oxford Radcliffe Hospitals NHS Trust and will occupy the Radcliffe Infirmary site during the year 2006. Currently with eighteen thousand students and several other sites locally, Oxford Brookes University is the fastest growing and largest student population in Oxford.

More about Douglas Gresham

Dougie had a healthy appetite for money and would carry out any challenge that he had thrust upon him with gusto. One example of this was that, on one occasion, whilst we were playing together in the barn, I had filled a galvanised bucket with cold water and dropped in three pennies. The challenge was to stand on his head in the bucket of water and I agreed to let him have the pennies if he did so. The words had no sooner left my mouth than Dougie was up on his hands, one either side of the bucket with his head now at the bottom of it – a perfect handstand! He got up with the water draining from his mop of near shoulder-length mousey coloured hair, shook his head, bent down and picked up the money from the bottom of the bucket.

On another occasion, he had arrived home from Magdalen College School dressed in his school uniform. We were stood at the edge of the lake near an old elm tree that had fallen many years ago with the branches reaching down into the water like the roots of a well-established mango tree. I said, 'Dougie, I bet you two shillings [that was twenty-four pennies and a lot of money for me then] that you won't run along the tree fully clothed in your school uniform and jump in the lake.' Gosh, no sooner said than done, he was up on the tree, he ran to the end about twenty feet away and 'splosh' he was in the water. Suddenly, he was lashing out and fighting his way through the water to get back to the edge of the lake where he managed to haul himself up the bank. As he stood up, shaking himself like the old poodle that Lewis had around the house, he immediately demanded the money, which I paid to him there and then. Dougie ran down to the house and told Jack that he had slipped and fallen into the lake! With today's technology washing machines, tumble driers and launderettes I suppose it would be no big deal but can you imagine what must have been going through Jacks mind. This 'urchin' was standing before him in what was probably the only school uniform he had, yet never a cross word – he really did love Dougie.

To get access to Dougie's bedroom we would have to go in from the back door (the tradesman's entrance) and through the kitchen. His bedroom wasn't that big and a small carpet was all he had to step out of bed onto, there were no such things as quilts in those days! Thinking back, and as you might expect I suppose, his bedroom was always untidy, the blankets on his bed in a heap looking as if he had lost a halfpenny and searched frantically to find it. A fishing rod stood in the corner of the room with its nylon line still threaded through the eyelets, the float and the hook, the remains of the bait – bread paste, maggots or dried worm – evidence of the last visit to the lake, still attached and secured in the cork handle by the hook. There was always a collection of comics, books, muddy shoes and boots, long socks rolled up in a ball still as he had taken them off, his school satchel, clothes never folded but quite literally strewn across the floor as he had removed them. Standing in the corner with the fishing rod were the guns that, quite likely, were still loaded.

Finally, the bomb. Dougie came home from school one day very excited about something he had learnt. 'Come on, Ron, let's find some weedkiller and I'll show you.' We found some weedkiller and then searched the old barn for what turned out to be a Tate and Lyle syrup tin, much like that of a coffee tin with a press lid. He tipped out the contents of the tin – nuts, bolts, washers etc. that Fred had collected over the years and part-filled it with the weedkiller. He then beckoned me to follow him to the kitchen of the former home where we searched for another material, a product readily available and used by some on a daily basis. When all was quiet, we stole the product from the kitchen cupboards and ran back to the barn where Dougie mixed the contents of the tin. He made a hole in the tin lid and tore off a strip of paraffin-soaked rag. He then pushed it through the hole to make a wick; he had made a bomb but I had no idea of just how powerful the device was!

Dougie put the device under the old Cotswold stone-type barn wall and said, 'When I light this, run.' As he lit the fuse we both ran and probably waited for three or four minutes before the explosion. We then crept back to see the damage. The stone wall was literally blown away. It was later that I learnt that this very mix of weedkiller and the product is what IRA terrorists were using in Northern Ireland against the British Army during the recent period of unrest and similar to the Oklahoma bombing in the USA. Although only a hundred yards or so away from the house, nobody enquired as to the noise of the explosion or as far as I know, even bothered to comment over the damage. Such was our freedom at the Kilns during the 1950s, that it shouldn't come as any surprise when I tell you that Dougie and I 'found' an old Austin 7 or Morris Minor, about a 1927 model, parked in a corner of the barn opposite the house. Today a collectors piece but in those days a gallon of petrol allowed us a unique opportunity to learn to drive the vehicle up and down the lane to the road (Kiln Lane). We had to reverse it back up to the house, but all was well until on one occasion Dougie reversed into a silver birch tree putting the shape of the tree into the rear of the vehicle at the roofline. We hurriedly parked the vehicle back in the corner of the barn and walked away!

Church Attendance

It is a fact that here in Britain we do not attend church to the extent of Lewis' day. A recent survey suggests that only 15 per cent of any parish attend on a regular basis. Churches are being sold off and turned into flats, houses and cafés, so if we are not very careful our place of worship, as we know it, will be gone forever. The words of C. S. Lewis will have no meaning in this country and all his good work to promote Christianity will be in vain. So what might happen then?

Was Lewis Chosen by God to Deliver to us All?

I have wondered many times how C. S. Lewis achieved his ability to write such powerful words, words that I have read, not understood, read again and sometimes still not understood. I have bookmarked a page and gone back to it several times before even beginning to get the message. So was this man naturally clever, gifted or was he receiving help? I ask a question for you all to ponder. Was this man specifically chosen by God to cleverly deliver to us all, because Lewis' books have sold over 200 million copies throughout the world – now that is some sermon!

Photographs, Descriptions and Tick Boxes

The purpose of the next section in this guide is to allow you to follow the C. S. Lewis Tour route by referring to the photographed landmarks as you proceed, with the author's brief description alongside. To record your own comments, thus acting as your diary for the day (which will be of great value when you get home), go to the blank pages at the back of the guide (Notes), because I can assure you that you will not remember it all. Tick the box to the right of the photographs as you progress through your own special world of *Narnia*.

Example: Photograph number one is of the Randolph Hotel in Beaumont Street, Oxford, from where the tour begins. You might like to record your visit to the Morse bar, or whether you managed to catch a glimpse of one of the rich and famous who frequent the hotel. An autograph in your personal guide would be a real prize! Remember also that some of the filming for *Shadowlands* took place here.

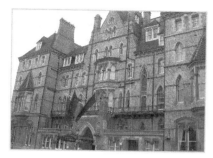

1.

The Randolph Hotel, Beaumont Street, from where the tour begins.

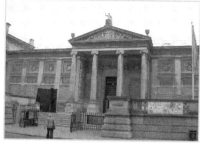

2.

The Ashmolean Museum, Beaumont Street, opposite the Randolph Hotel.

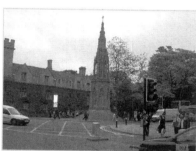

3.

Martyrs Memorial, St Giles. To the right of the traffic lights as you turn left into St Giles.

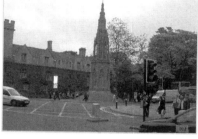

4.

St John's College on your right-hand side in St Giles.

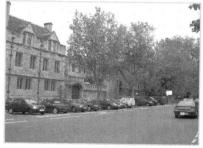

5.

The Eagle and Child, 49 St Giles. On your left opposite St John's College.

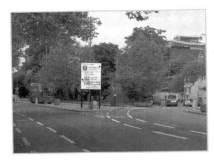

6.

Junction of Woodstock Road and Banbury Road. Take the right-hand fork into Banbury Road, with St Giles Church now on your left.

7.

The junction of Banbury Road and Norham Road, turn right here.

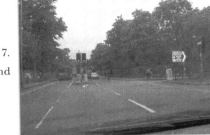

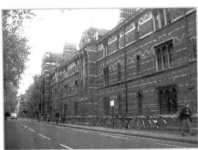

8.

Keble College is on your right-hand side.

9.

The Natural History Museum on your left-hand side.

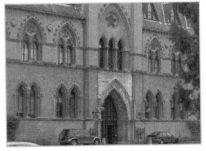

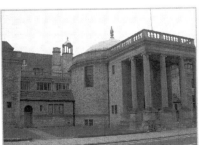

10.

Rhodes House on the right in South Parks Road

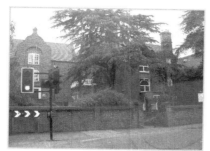

11.

Facing Linacre College, South Parks Road.

12.

Facing St Cross Church, Manor Road.

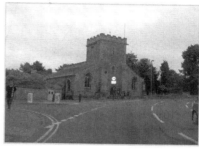

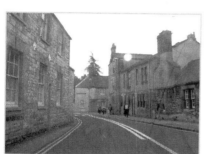

13.

Approach to Longwall Street. (Old City wall, between building on your right).

14.

Battlement style wall of Magdalen College on the left in Longwall Street.

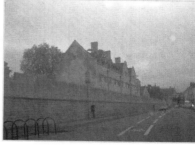

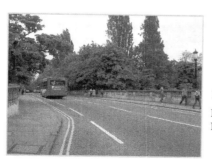

15.

Magdalen Bridge, where the May Day celebrations take place.

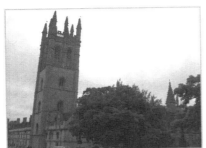

16.

Magdalen College Great Tower. The Magdalen College choir sing from the top of the tower at 6am on 1st May annually, as in the film *Shadowlands.*

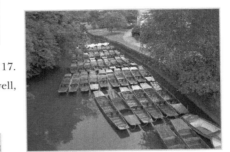

17.

Punts on the River Cherwell, under Magdalen Bridge.

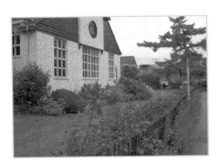

18.

Magdalen College School where the Gresham boys attended during the 1950s.

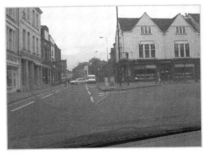

19.

The approach to St Clements towards Headington.

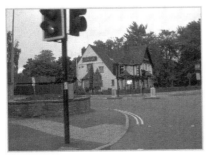

20.

Junction of Headley Way (White Horse public house on the left). Headington Road and London Roads merge here. Stay on London Road until you reach Sandfield Road a few hundred yards away on the left. Turn into Sandfield Road look for number 76 on the left.

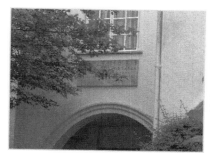

21.

The plaque above the garage at 76 Sandfield Road, Headington, confirms J. R. R. Tolkien lived here during the years 1953–68.

22.

Another photograph of J. R. R. Tolkien's former home, 76 Sandfield Road.

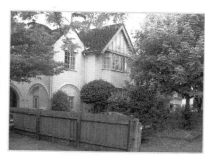

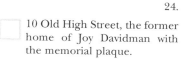

23.

Approach to Headington traffic lights, turn left into Old High Street.

24.

10 Old High Street, the former home of Joy Davidman with the memorial plaque.

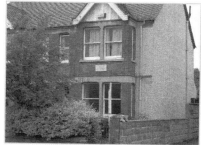

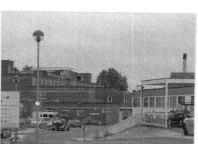

25.

The Nuffield Orthopaedic Centre, formerly the Wingfield Hospital where Joy was admitted to hospital months after their marriage.

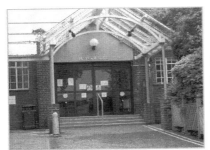

26.

Entrance to the Mayfair Suite (Jack and Joy's marriage was blessed in a bedside ceremony here).

27.

Crossroads at Old Road, Headington Quarry. Cross over into Old Road. Taking the second turn on the left, continue for six hundred yards.

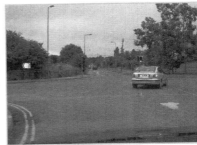

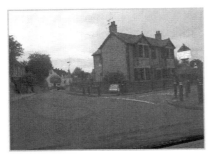

28.

Turn right at Quarry Hollow, continue for two hundred yards.

29.

Approach to Quarry School Place, turn right taking 'S' bend.

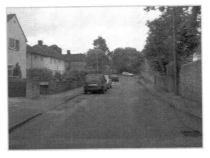

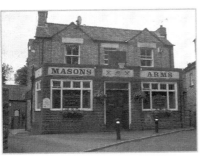

30.

Facing the Masons Arms, another former Lewis watering hole, bear right.

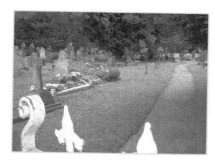

31.

Entrance to Holy Trinity Church and churchyard.

32.

Holy Trinity Church.

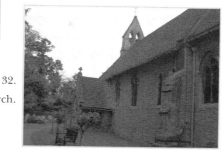

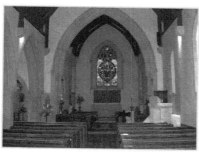

33.

Inside Holy Trinity Church

34.

A view of the Pulpit from where Jack and Warnie habitually sat.

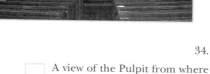

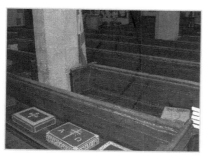

35.

The Lewis 'pew'. Jack sat near the pillar to St George, Warnie on the outside.

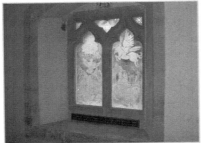

36.

The Narnia Window in Holy Trinity Church.

37.

C. S. Lewis memorabilia at the rear of Holy Trinity Church. Please deposit cash in the offerings safe on the left of the door as you exit. Follow the narrow footpath in front of you towards the C. S. Lewis grave sign, affixed to the stone wall.

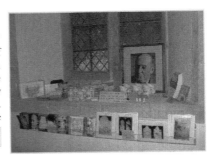

38.

The Lewis brothers' tombstone. The sixth tombstone along under the tall pine trees.

39.

Lewis' tombstone in the foreground, Don Tackley pays his respects to an Italian killed in action during the war, with Holy Trinity Church in the background.

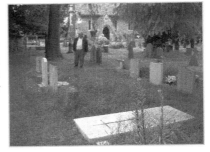

40.

With your left shoulder at the head of the Lewis brothers' tombstone, look to the right of their grave for the grave of the two Mrs Moores.

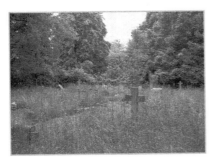

41.

Sadly, the unkempt grave of the two Mrs Moores.

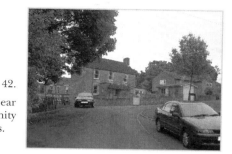

42.

As you leave Holy Trinity Church bear right taking the slight incline into Trinity Road, continue on two hundred yards.

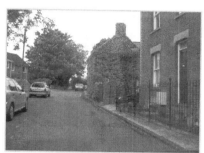

43.

Approaching the dual carriageway from Trinity Road.

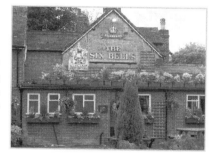

44.

With the Six Bells public house on your left, turn right to face the dual carriage way, and then left towards the roundabout.

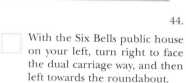

45.

Approaching Headington roundabout, also known locally as Green Road roundabout.

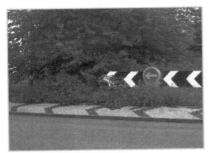

46.

Headington roundabout, take the fourth exit towards Beckley ☐

47.

St Mary's Church, Bayswater Road.

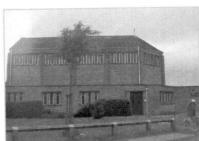

48.

Travelling down Bayswater Road towards Oxford Crematorium. ☐

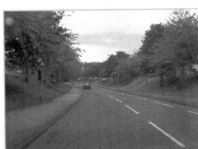

49.

☐ Entrance to Oxford Crematorium on the left-hand side.

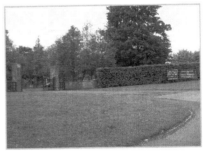

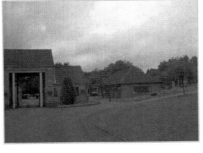

50. ☐

Crematorium Chapels to the left. Chapel of Remembrance, waiting room and toilets to your right (the toilet/rest room will close at 4pm).

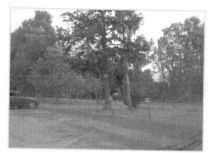

51.

Park on the right-hand side but not in the reserved bays please.

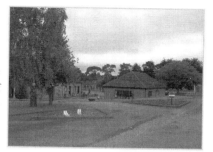

52.

Walk towards the Chapel of Remembrance and waiting room, keeping to the right-hand side.

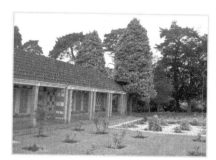

53.

Cloister 2 in the bottom left-hand corner, walk towards the two leylandi trees on the right.

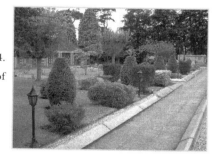

54.

Approaching the Garden of Rembrance near Cloister 2.

Remember
HELEN JOY
DAVIDMAN
D. July 1960
Loved wife of
C. S. LEWIS

Here the whole world (stars, water, air,
And field, and forest, as they were
Reflected in a single mind)
Like cast off clothes was left behind
In ashes, yet with hope that she,
Re-born from holy poverty,
In lenten lands, hereafter may
Resume them on her Easter Day

55.

The memorial plaque to Helen Joy Davidman.

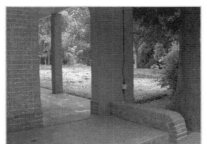

56.

Walk through this archway to see the area in which Joy Lewis' ashes were scattered (Joy was cremated in the name of Mrs Joy Lewis, despite the plaque reading Remember Helen Joy Davidman).

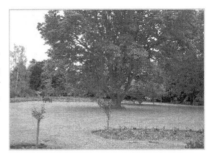

57.

Head for the large oak trees and the bench seats, until you have the four magnolia trees on your right hand side.

58.

Rose bed B4 is now on the bottom left-hand side. The ashes of Mrs Joy Lewis were scattered between B4 and the magnolia trees.

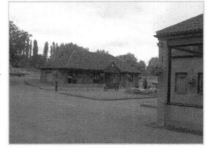

59.

On leaving Cloister 2, or the area in which Joy's ashes were scattered you will be facing the Chapel of Remembrance and the waiting room.

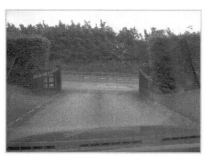

60.

Leave Oxford Crematorium via the exit gate, as opposed to the entrance gate when you arrived.

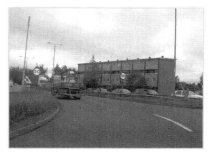

61.

At Headington roundabout take the A4142 for Cowley (Ring Road).

62.

The slip road approach to Risinghurst Estate, turn left.

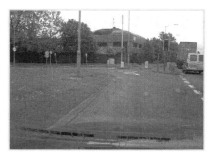

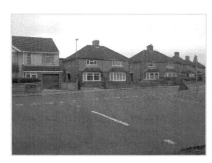

63.

Facing Green Road and Kiln Lane, turn right.

64.

The original entrance to the Kilns was between the mature trees and the fence on the right, just eight or nine feet in width and with no kerb stones.

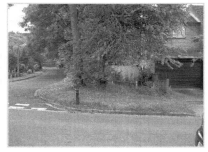

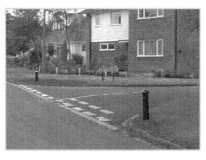

65.

Approach to Lewis Close, a cul-de-sac.

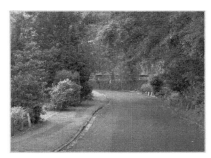

66.

A view of Lewis' former home in the background, from the area that was once an orchard

67.

The tradesman's entrance to the Kilns where bread, post, milk etc.would be delivered.

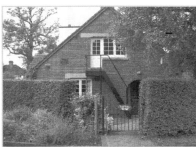

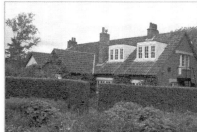
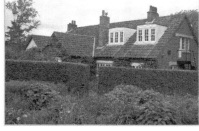

68.

The front view of C. S. Lewis' former home

69.

The narrow muddy footpath leading to the C. S. Lewis Reserve and lake. (This was all once part of Lewis' eight-acre garden.)

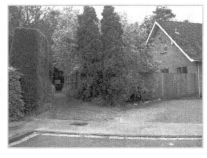

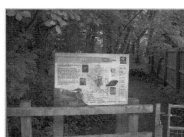

70.

Entrance to the C. S. Lewis Reserve (in memory of Henry Stephen). Turn left after the gate and make your way through the woodland to find the air-raid shelter built by Fred Paxford. Continue along the muddy path to the lake.

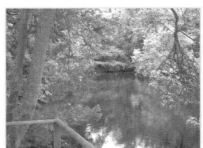

71.

The lake, also once part of Lewis' back garden!

72.

As you leave Lewis Close turn right to see number 6 Grovelands Road, where this author was born, just two hundred yards away! Turn left into Collinwood Road.

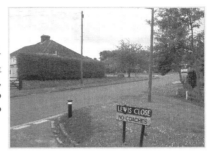

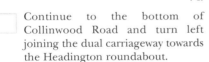

73.

The Ampleforth Arms public house, another Lewis/Tolkien watering hole from where Dougie and I fetched the beer in empty cider bottles.

74.

Continue to the bottom of Collinwood Road and turn left joining the dual carriageway towards the Headington roundabout.

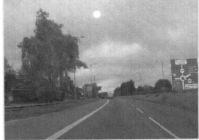

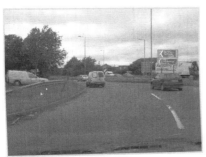

75.

Leaving the Headington roundabout take the A40 North (fourth exit).

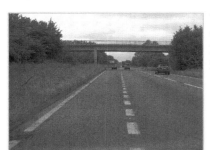

76.

The Marston flyover. Take the slip road here and turn left within two hundred yards.

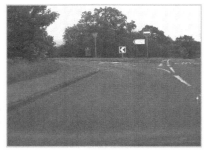

77.

Follow the road for two hundred yards and turn right into Marsh Lane towards Oxford city.

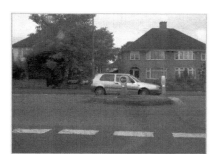

78.

Facing the mini roundabout with Cherwell Drive to the left and Marston Ferry Road to your right, turn right heading towards Oxford city (north).

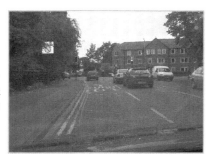

79.

Approaching Banbury Road, turn left towards Oxford city. Continue for one and a half miles.

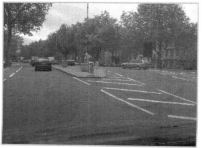

80.

Approaching St Giles thoroughfare. The Eagle and Child public house will now be on your right-hand side behind the trees and the Randolph Hotel, from where your tour started, is situated a few hundred yards further along on the right in Beaumont Street, and opposite Martyrs Memorial.